SAFE ON THE DOOR

THE COMPLETE GUIDE FOR DOOR SUPERVISORS

LEE MORRISON

Hodder Arnold

A MEMBER OF THE HODDER HEADLINE GROUP

First published in Great Britain in 2006 by
Hodder Education, a member of the Hodder Headline Group,
338 Euston Road, London NW1 3BH

www.hoddereducation.co.uk

Hodder Headline's policy is to use papers that are natural, renewable and
recyclable products and made from wood grown in sustainable forests.
The logging and manufacturing processes are expected to conform to the
environmental regulations of the country of origin.

The advice and information in this book are believed to be true and
accurate at the date of going to press, but neither the authors nor the publisher
can accept any legal responsibility or liability for any errors or omissions.

British Library Cataloguing in Publication Data
A catalogue record for this book is available from the British Library

ISBN-10 0 340 90575 1
ISBN-13 978 0 340 90575 3

1 2 3 4 5 6 7 8 9 10

Typeset in 10 on 12pt Palatino by Phoenix Photosetting, Chatham, Kent
Printed and bound in the UK by Martins the Printer, Berwick upon Tweed

What do you think about this book? Or any other Hodder
Education title? Please send your comments to the feedback
section on www.hoddereducation.co.uk.

CONTENTS

FOREWORD

The role of door supervisor has always been a challenging one. I have to say that in my 45 years on this spinning blue planet it has been the hardest – yet most rewarding – job I have ever undertaken. I have experienced people at their very best and their very worst. Four of my friends were murdered during my ten years in the job; many more were badly injured, some ended up in prison and one or two found themselves on the psychiatrist's couch as a result of over-exposure to violence. It is not a job for the faint of heart.

Things have changed a great deal since I first wore my tuxedo and stood under the glow of nightclub neon, way back in the 1980s. And I'm delighted that they have. In the bad old days there was an excess of violence and a plethora of bloody battles that often spilled from the beer-sticky dance floor out onto the pavement arena when hard men turned their hard drinking into hard fighting. The problem was, as far as I can see, in those days there was absolutely no alliance (other than a perfunctory 'unholy' one) between the doormen and the police. So when violence reared its ugly head we dealt with it – on the front door or inside the club – immediately, often brutally, and never (ever) considered calling the police for assistance, because a call to the judiciary meant a black mark in the register and the threat of losing your drinks licence. Although no one really wanted to admit it back then, bouncers (as we were called) were hired more to protect the licence of the club than to protect the customers, the staff or the property. And a closed club was anathema to owners, managers, employees and customers alike – you can't ply trade with a bolted front door and a 'closed' notice in the local paper. In those days the police hated the doormen, the doormen hated the police, and neither respected the important and often thankless role played by the other.

I am delighted to say that this is all starting to change now and the role of door supervisor – while admittedly still in its transitional stages – is at last getting the respect and kudos it deserves. And, more often than not, door staff work as a cohesive unit with their local constabulary to keep order when anarchy (or even just an argument) threatens. No longer the knuckle-dragging Neanderthal, bouncing heads like pinballs and notching up fights on a metaphoric gun barrel, the door supervisor of today is increasingly likely to be an articulate postgraduate working his way through university, a single mum doing a difficult but legitimate part-time job, or a self-defence expert looking for some pragmatic experience in the art of fighting without fighting.

Lee Morrison is leading this new wave of thinking door supervisor, and he should be applauded for that. His book is filled with life-saving advice, useful and effective (and legal) self-defence techniques, tips on developing the correct mind-set with exercises in mental conditioning, details of the constraints of the law, and much, much more. This book is a delight – an Aladdin's cave of gems that might one day prove life-saving.

I wish it had been in print when I first started on the doors – I'd definitely have been better prepared because of it.

Geoff Thompson
2005

ABOUT THE AUTHOR

I was born in south-east London during the latter part of the
1960s. My mum was a single parent on a low income and we had
no home of our own so we moved around a lot. To me this meant
lots of different schools and always being the new kid. This
allowed me to experience bullying of all shapes and sizes – all
equally unpleasant – which in turn meant that I needed to learn
how to defend myself. And that's where I began training in and
studying combat – a personal journey that has now spanned
some 24 years. Over the years I have trained in Chinese,
Japanese, Thai and Filipino weapon systems, western boxing and
wrestling, as well as various methods of close-quarter combat
and defensive tactics, which I now teach full time. At the age of
23 I threw myself into strength training and weight lifting in an
attempt to increase my size and strength.

I continued with this for the following ten years, trying my hand at competitive lifting, with
notable success at amateur level. Of course, training in all forms of combat has been a
wonderful education as well as an opportunity to meet and train with some of the best
people in the world, many of whom I am proud to call my friends. It was around the same
time that I started working as a pub and nightclub doorman. It was the beginning of the
1990s and the era of the bouncer was just coming to a close, being replaced by the new (at
the time) door supervisor and badge scheme. As I mention elsewhere in this book, the job of
doorman has seen many changes over the decades – from the days of the 'chuck-out man' to
the modern door supervisor. One thing that hasn't changed, though, is man's capacity for
violence, and I've got to tell you that it was only when I started working on the doors that
my study and training (in terms of what I've found works for me in a 'live' situation) was
really tested – and it was a steep learning curve. I found it a massive test of character (and it
still is at times). All of a sudden there was this drastic need to chip away quickly at all the
non-essentials, and whittle down everything I had learnt so far to no more than one or two
good methods that had worked for me on more than one occasion. In over a decade
working on the doors, I have learned an awful lot about myself, and about the way I
respond under pressure.

I also feel that I have – at least as far as my work is concerned – managed to sort the wheat
from the chaff regarding the fighting arts I've studied so far. For the past five years I have
been studying 'western combatives', which are methods based on the teachings of the great
hand-to-hand combat instructors of old. I have a great passion for this stuff – not just the
physical techniques but the history of it all too. Of course, more important than techniques
are the concepts of avoidance where and when possible; and, if in danger, the need to be
pre-emptive, training for impact and learning all you can about the adrenal response.

All this has been said and written about before, by bigger and better people than me. I have
merely come to similar conclusions as the result of similar experience. It can all be summed

up with the following quote from a great author whose name escapes me: 'Thirty seconds on the sidewalk is worth three years in the dojo.'

I now spend most of my time writing, training, and teaching self-protection and personal security skills through my company the Urban Combatives Self-Protection Association. I teach people who work in the public sector, and the staff of door and event security companies in and around the south of England, as well as various combative groups up and down the country.

Lee Morrison
2005

ACKNOWLEDGMENTS

Every effort has been made to trace and acknowledge ownership of copyright. The publishers will be glad to make suitable arrangements with any copyright holders whom it has not been possible to contact.

The author and publishers would like to thank the following for the use of photographs in this volume:

Patrick Giardino/CORBIS, front cover; Nabil Elderkin/Stone/Getty Images, Figure 1.1; John Powell Photographer/Alamy, Figure 2.1; Robert Battersby/BDI Images, Figure 2.2; Lino Wchima/Photographers Direct, Figure 2.3; Simon Belcher/Alamy, Figure 2.4; Elvele Images/Alamy, Figure 3.3; Photofusion Picture Library/Alamy, Figure 3.4; EGON/Alamy, Figure 4.1 (left); Channel Island Pictures/Alamy, Figure 4.1 (right); BSIP, CHASSENET/SCIENCE PHOTO LIBRARY, Figure 10.1; Paul Doyle/Alamy, Figure 11.1; David Michael Zimmerman/CORBIS, Figure 11.2; Everynight Images/Alamy, Figure 12.1; Matthew Smith/PYMCA, Figure 13.1

Original photography by James Newell.

INTRODUCTION

The idea behind this book is to provide men and women (both veterans and new recruits), working within the field of door and event security under the title now referred to as 'door supervisor', with as deep an insight as possible into the exciting and often murky world of the bouncer. This insight is offered in a two-pronged way because I feel it is my responsibility to provide the reader with as much information as possible from both sides of the coin.

The first side, therefore, refers to the latest current legislation as laid down by the Security Industry Authority (SIA). This is basically the crux of the Level 2 National Certificate for Door Supervisor's manual – a volume with which all those who have experience of the new SIA national licensing scheme will already be familiar. In my opinion, the manual does cover the essential need-to-know aspects of the job and, as dry as you might find it to study, it is essential reading. For this reason, Unit 1 of said manual will be touched upon here, and the training and knowledge it provides should be studied by any and all within the industry.

The other side of the coin – and the core of this book – however, is the reality of door work, what the SIA refers to as the 'conflict management' side. This is where my opinion may cause some degree of controversy, but trust me when I say that any veteran door person worth their salt will know exactly where I am coming from. The resources I drew upon while writing this book come from over a decade of personal experience working on the doors in various venues all over the south of England, including London, Portsmouth and Southampton, and also from my peers, people considered extremely experienced particularly within the realm of dealing with real violence.

This includes input from veteran door people who have been in the job long enough to relate their experiences from active learning, along with comments and advice from others working within the field of close protection, security and law enforcement. The advice given will always, where possible, seek to give the reader a non-physical option, but please bear in mind that sometimes this will not be possible and there is no doubt that if you choose this kind of employment you will at some point have to deal with violence – in the physical sense of the term.

It is my personal opinion – and I know a lot of people who have done this job for years who are inclined to agree – that Unit 2 of the SIA manual, which attempts to deal with the conflict management side of things, is woefully inadequate in terms of offering the door supervisor any functional means by which to deal with what is, hopefully in your town at least, the gratuitously violent minority. Before the SIA licensing regulations came into force we had a badge scheme monitored by each borough's local council. It was common knowledge then that most councils frowned upon the idea of offering any physical self-protection skills to door supervisors; they could not be seen to advocate violence in any way, even for the sake of self-preservation. I can see the same thing in the new legislation, but unfortunately burying your head in the sand and ignoring the reality of the problem will not make the violence go away – it will still be encountered and will still have to be controlled and dealt with.

It is therefore my objective to offer the reader some tried and tested physical options should all else fail. Of course, one cannot learn purely from a book, so you will need to find a like-minded individual and practise in the physical sense, or where possible seek out some professional instruction (see the 'Further training' section at the end of this book). What follows are some tried and tested ideas to help make this often dangerous job a little more manageable and effective.

Achieving the mind-set needed to make you efficient in this line of work will require some planning and practice – and will include practising the physical options we are bound to touch on in a manual of this kind. But more important than this are additional street-smart skills like awareness and observation, understanding body language and pre-conflict indicators, as well as the need to cultivate 'people skills', learn verbal de-escalation methods, and so on. As I have already said, you should always seek to employ the non-physical option where possible – the days of the bully-boy bouncer are long gone. This is the era of the door supervisor, a security professional who is there to protect work colleagues and paying customers, as well as him/herself, from the antisocial behaviour that is a fact of life in society today. This may involve an array of duties that we will look at in some detail as we go along, the most frequent of which is likely to be dealing with aggressive behaviour and violence. For this reason, the aim of this book is to help you become capable and effective at controlling this element by devising a workable game plan that will allow you to deal with any and all situations you may face in the pub/nightclub environment.

Make no mistake, though – only active learning through personal experience is what will mould you into a capable door supervisor. So time must be served, and the reliable feeling of the adrenalin rush must be experienced and controlled. If you are to become at all proficient in this line of work it is essential that, no matter how difficult it becomes, you must return to it night after night. Of course, you might consider working the door for no other reason than to supplement your income with a few quid, in which case you are likely to take only a half-hearted interest in how you do the job … but I could think of easier jobs to do for that extra bit of cash. In fact, I would go so far as to say that most jobs are more appealing than that of door supervisor, especially when it all goes tits-up on a Friday night and you find yourself facing some bottle-wielding Neanderthal who wants to introduce you to some ugly violence for no other reason than 'because he can'.

Try working the door in some areas of the country where the management make stab-vests for door staff compulsory and you will soon get your head round what I'm talking about. In such circumstances, when actually faced with a potentially violent situation, most of us would rather be anywhere else in the world than right there at that moment. During my years on the door I met people from all walks of life, and I worked in all sorts of places, from the very respectable to the extremely undesirable and everything in between, and I often heard the comment 'You got an easy number there, mate – what do you get, 60 quid a night for just standing there? Money for old rope.' In reality even in those nice, quiet and respectable places, the potential for violence will exist. In fact, wherever you find people and alcohol you have a recipe for trouble, and that's without adding drugs or mental health to the equation.

Even on those quiet nights when everything goes without a hitch, most door staff will agree that you earn your money in the shape of tired feet, spates of boredom and a weary mind from staying switched on all night. But then, of course, there are the occasions when it all kicks off – believe me when I say that at times like that you feel like you've earned your whole year's money in one night, especially if there have been multiple incidents.

My intention in writing this book, then, is to provide you with some thoughts and practical methods that I found to be effective during my time in the job. The job of the door supervisor is now harder to perform than ever before: you will constantly find yourself placed in situations where you will have to make split-second decisions that will hopefully be the correct ones that will allow you a maintenance level of personal security while preserving a high degree of professionalism.

Your actions will be looked at under a microscope that will require justification for them and their consequences if they are inappropriate. The new national door supervisor qualification, which is manifesting itself in the form of a licence obtained via a training course, has created a totally different kind of perspective from that prevalent in the days of the bouncer, and does not even remotely reflect how things used to be.

How can any youngster without any real experience of life, let alone of working the doors, gain the respect of the 'old-school bouncer' who has probably dealt with more violent confrontation than he cares to remember? Of course, like anything else, this has its pros and cons. I agree that there was a need to find a way to eliminate the minority element of bullying and criminal activity that on occasion reared its head within the murky world of the bouncer. The move by local councils towards introducing their own schemes, and now the SIA's development of a nationally recognised licence, has helped to monitor and eliminate many a bad apple that served to sour the image of the bouncer. However, such steps have done away with many a good egg, too, who was capable and experienced at dealing with the worst of the minority elements that frequent our pubs and clubs with a view to creating havoc, misconduct and gratuitous violence. A large percentage of those that have replaced them are young people with good intentions who can now get 'badged up' after a very short training course – but what, may I ask, is the end result in terms of public safety and quality of work?

There have been many changes throughout the history of the bouncer. Some of my peers who worked the doors in the 1960s and 1970s have related how times have altered since then. The same can be said of the 1980s through to the beginning of the 1990s, when I started, which saw the slow but progressive change from the days of the chuck-out man/bouncer into the formative years of the door supervisor. And coming right up to date, we've moved on to the latest phase, looked at in detail here. As a profession, it certainly doesn't stand still. So, regardless of whether you are new to this profession or a time-served veteran, please read this book with an open mind. It depicts these changes as they've developed and will hopefully, in some way or another, act as a supplement to the personal learning experience of actually doing the job. After all, there is no better training for the event than the event itself.

The information presented in this book is garnered from the real-life experience of men and women who have done the job of what is now referred to as door supervisor for years. In the main, it is information that has been gathered via intuition and practical experience, forged in an often very violent and aggressive environment. Some of the ideas you will read about in this book come from veteran doormen that I have worked and trained with. There is also input from people involved in law enforcement and individuals that I consider to have had a lot more experience than me in the field of physical confrontation. Much of the information is also based on the knowledge I have acquired over 25 years of training in various combative arts, and gleaned from the physical and psychological confrontations I have had and learned from over the years – from the days of the school playground right up to the present day. These include quite a few situations within door and security work, and it is situations such as these – which, I might add, were all occasions where I had done my utmost to avoid violence, but to no avail – that have formed the basis of the most character-building employment I have experienced thus far. From all my past experiences, and from lessons learned from my peers, I have absorbed what I have found useful for me. May I suggest that, as I said above, you read this offering with an open mind and do likewise.

Please note that the ideas and techniques presented here have been tried and tested under pressure – some are based on my own experience and others on that of my peers, from whom I have learned a great deal. However, they are merely *suggestions*.

It is important to remember that all actions carry consequences. The consequences of violence in any environment, door work included, can be tragically negative: heavy fines, imprisonment, serious injury and even death are all real possibilities. Please strive to seek non-violent solutions wherever possible – that, after all, is what real self-defence is all about.

Stay safe, and thank you for your time.

PART ONE
RESPONSIBILITIES OF THE DOOR SUPERVISOR

CHAPTER ONE

RESPONSIBILITIES AND BEHAVIOUR

1.1 Definition of duties

The main duty of the door supervisor working within the leisure industry is to make sure that the customers who frequent the venue in question have an enjoyable time in a safe environment. The object of the training qualification for a national licence for door supervisors is to provide the knowledge and understanding necessary for the role of door supervisor. The list below gives ten examples of the duties that you as a door supervisor are expected to carry out (each supervisor should be briefed as to their responsibilities in each particular area). It is a guideline duty profile as laid down by the Security Industry Authority (SIA), which has responsibility for the licensing of door supervisors.

Roles and responsibility

To ensure that a safe, friendly environment is maintained at your designated point of duty at all times throughout the event:

1. monitor the patrons throughout the venue and take any action deemed necessary to ensure patrons' safety and security
2. prevent overcrowding throughout the venue and ensure that queuing systems are maintained and, where needed, search procedures are carried out
3. prevent patrons from climbing on structures/stages
4. keep all fire exits clear and comply with health and safety regulations
5. identify incidents among patrons and report them accordingly
6. continually monitor the crowd's movements and ensure that in the event of any disorder or unsafe situations arising, appropriate action is taken
7. know the layout of the site, fire procedures and first-aid points
8. be conversant with emergency messages and evacuation routes
9. recognise potential fire hazards and suspect packages, and report any findings to a supervisor/event control
10. maintain a high level of customer care and respond positively to customer complaints.

At times there will be cause to reprimand customers for unacceptable behaviour, handle complaints and disputes over service (e.g. between customer and bar staff) and defuse domestic disputes between customers, as well as intervene and handle all other arguments and physical fights. You will also be required to refuse entry politely, carry out search procedures for drugs, weapons and other prohibited items, and evict people for unacceptable behaviour such as fighting.

A good crew will have a plan of action ready in the event of a fire, an injured patron, a stolen purse or any degree of violence – from an escalating argument between two mates to an all-out kick-off. Having a plan in place is a lot more functional than trying to work under pressure with no direction. Above all, you should never compromise your own safety for the benefit of the client. In potentially dangerous situations, which threaten personal safety, always summon assistance before getting involved. An employee's safety is of paramount importance.

One duty that is most certainly *not* in the job description of a door supervisor, though expected by some employers, is that of glass collecting. If you are asked to perform this duty, don't do it. It is dangerous for any member of security staff to be moving through a crowd collecting a tower of glasses. All it takes is for someone that you've had a previous grievance with to shove you over and you will end up cut to pieces. Bar staff don't do door work and door supervisors don't collect glasses. Period!

Of course, moving the odd bottle or glass out of harm's way is always a sensible thing to do; for one thing it cuts down on any weapon potential should a problem arise. The broken beer glass or bottle is the favoured edged weapon of the pub/club environment (see Section 9.3). Some establishments will use only plastic, but unfortunately these are in the minority. Most places use glass, which in my opinion makes our job a lot more dangerous. You only have to look at the kind of horrific injuries sustained by someone who has been glassed in a pub fight to realise the danger of their use in such a volatile environment.

The SIA, local authorities and the police are all working towards reducing crime and disorder in and around licensed premises; as a door supervisor you are part of that strategy. That said, never forget that your personal safety is a priority. Yes, you must strive to work as part of a strong functional team, and to the criteria laid down, but at the end of the day you are the person most responsible for your own welfare – so remember that your safety is your priority, stay switched on, look out for other members of your team, and don't take any unnecessary risks dictated by bravado or ego.

1.2 Behaviour and conduct

Adhere to the appropriate dress code. Display your in-date SIA-approved badge at all times while on duty. Conduct yourself in an orderly and professional manner in the workplace and refrain from any horseplay. If you are the kind of door supervisor who leans against the door with a cigarette in your mouth, chatting on your mobile phone, then you are not projecting the ideal image. Nor should you become the type of person who walks into the job feeling as if you have some kind of power – all full of your own importance – as this means you amount to nothing more than a bully with a badge. Instead, you must learn to communicate with people and exude the manner of a confident, helpful professional.

Your authority to carry out your duties comes direct from the licensee, or the venue's management working on behalf of the licensee. You are therefore helping to carry out the duties attached to the venue's licence(s). The SIA qualification covers this under the heading 'Codes of Behaviour', and it deals with four areas: personal appearance, professional attitude and skills, general conduct, and company standards.

Figure 1.1 Remain professional at all times

Basically you need to adhere to the points already mentioned, and take an honest look at yourself and decide if you are representing yourself and your company in a positive light with a real sense of professionalism. How do you look? How do you talk to others? These two factors can make a major difference to how you are perceived and treated by others. Remember: you never get a second chance to make a good first impression.

1.3 Attitude and communication skills

Attitude and communication are the two main factors associated with customer relations and people skills. How you are perceived by the customer is very important: it is an accepted fact that whether or not staff display a friendly and helpful demeanour will have a bearing on whether a paying customer returns to a venue.

As a door supervisor you are the first person the customer sees when deciding whether to come into your venue or to go elsewhere; you are also the last person they see when they leave at the end of the night, so how you look and how you speak to all patrons really does matter – right from the start. Always strive to be polite and speak in a clear and understandable tone.

Try to treat all patrons equally and treat everyone with respect. Speaking from a position of over a decade of time-served experience, I can tell you that the better your people skills, the easier you will find your job within this field.

Of course, you should never get too familiar and must focus on your duties as a professional. However, as any door supervisor worth their salt will tell you, the people you serve on the door can be assets to you or they can be liabilities, and developing a positive rapport with the customer can go a long way towards achieving good customer relations and defusing hostility. People should leave your venue with the feeling that they have been treated fairly and with respect. So strive to be a good representative for your profession and give your customers a positive impression of the role of the door supervisor.

CHAPTER TWO

THE LAW IN RELATION TO DOOR SUPERVISORS

2.1 You and the law

It is one of your main duties as a door supervisor to make sure that laws are not broken within your venue. The areas of most relevance in terms of the law are:

- licensing
- public entertainment
- drug misuse and drug dealing
- sex discrimination
- disability discrimination
- race relations.

The purpose of the laws relating to these areas is to ensure that no one is treated unfairly on the grounds of sex, race or disability (see also Section 2.8), and to ensure that patrons keep within the law in relation to licensing and other legislation.

The four types of law

There are four basic types of law:

1. civil law
2. criminal law
3. common law
4. statute law.

We will now take a brief look at each of these in turn.

Civil law

Civil law helps govern everyday life and may relate to less serious offences such as trespass or domestic disputes.

Criminal law

Criminal law deals with more serious matters. The criminal law of England and Wales comes from two sources: common law and statute law, described below.

Common law

Common law is law that is not the result of legislation. Instead it has developed as a result of the customs of the people over many years, which have then been justified and developed further by the decisions and rulings of judges.

Statute law

Statute law is written law, passed by the Houses of Parliament and given Royal Assent. It lays down specific offences that are violations of this law. Such violations are punishable through criminal courts. Examples of criminal offences include theft, damage, drugs supply and assault. As a door supervisor, it is important that you understand the law in relation to violent incidents.

The following is a list of some of the types of assault you may come across in your work.

- **Common assault:** when a person or people fight but neither party has sustained any injuries such as cuts and bruises. This is not an arrestable offence.
- **Actual bodily harm (ABH):** when an assault leads to actual injury.
- **Grievous bodily harm (GBH):** when an assault leads to serious injury such as broken bones.
- **ABH or GBH with intent:** an example of this offence would be when an individual can be shown to have carried out an assault on another person with the intention of doing them harm – for example, picking up a heavy ashtray and using it to injure someone else would indicate intent.
- **Assault on a police officer:** any assault of this nature is seen as a more serious offence.
- **Racially aggravated assault:** an assault on a person (or persons) accompanied by racial insults or in any way motivated by racism.
- **Indecent assault:** an assault of a sexual nature inflicted on a man or woman by a man or woman.

All of the above classes of assault, except common assault, are arrestable offences.

2.2 Use of force

Reasonable and necessary force

Door supervisors may have to use physical force in the course of their duties. Such force must be no more than is reasonable and necessary (see the 'Warning' box). Use of force above and beyond what is strictly reasonable and necessary could result in prosecution for assault. *The use of any force should be avoided if at all possible.*

Your authority

There are no easy rules about when to use force in your work and how much to use, but remember that your actions may lead to prosecution. The authority given to you by the licensee of the venue to control customers' movements or behaviour does not apply off the premises.

> ## WARNING
>
> If injury is caused as a result of the force you have used, you could be accused of assault. The police and the courts will have to decide whether you have used more than reasonable and necessary force. If you did use too much force, you could be convicted of assault. Any act of force could result in the police investigating your conduct, which may lead to prosecution.

Using too much force has given door supervisors a bad reputation in the past. According to the SIA you are working in the modern leisure industry. Customers come to your venue to enjoy themselves; they look to you to ensure their safety. If they see you using too much force, even if they are not involved, they are likely to feel threatened. This is not good for you or the venue.

That's quite understandable but, when all's said and done, let's not forget just how dangerous it really is for anyone working in a field that requires them to deal with violence on a day-to-day basis. For this reason, your own personal safety in real circumstances of danger should always remain your priority, and it is important to have a grasp of the most current laws regarding self-protection. The following section offers some information on this subject.

Pre-emptive use of force

The law supports the use of pre-emptive force where it is both reasonable and necessary. Such use of force, in the right circumstances, can be used as a defence in a court of law. The courts have stated in the past that for a person to wait to be attacked and consequently injured before taking action is not self-defence at all. Self-defence is not about waiting to be hurt – if you wait for confirmation that you will be attacked, that confirmation is likely to arrive in the form of an injury to you. If someone breaks a beer glass on the corner of a table and proceeds to lunge at you with it, you would not be expected to wait for the attack actually to take place and would be perfectly justified in using a pre-emptive strike. In such situations, where you have the *honest belief that you are in danger of serious injury or worse* (remember those words), then pre-emptive use of force is acceptable, provided that no more force than is reasonable in the circumstances is employed to repel the attack. If, as a door supervisor, you consider the fact that every time you use force against another person you may well have to justify your actions, then you should always be able to act reasonably.

Just remember: if you do not genuinely fear for your safety, then you are not legally or morally justified to strike first. If you overreact in terms of the deliberate amount of force you use, and you are aware of the fact, then you will more than likely have to answer to the police and possibly even a court of law. If it comes to that, here are some examples of the kinds of question you are likely to be asked.

- Was there a need to use force/did you strive to employ non-physical options?
- Was there a major difference in size and build between you and the said individual(s)?
- Were any weapons involved?
- Were you potentially facing more than one aggressor?

- At what stage did you stop your use of force?
- Did you employ the use of force as a last resort, in good faith, or was it in any way malicious on your part?

What is deemed 'reasonable use of force' in such a stressful scenario will always be something of a grey area. Circumstances like this are never black and white, but from a moral standpoint, as long as you do what you deem reasonable under the circumstances and you adhere to the above advice, then you should be all right.

These days, there is most certainly no room for bullies in this field of employment; and, hopefully, the majority of conflict situations you are likely to face will be resolved without physical action. However, make no mistake, out there in the real world is a minority that will leave you with no alternative to a physical response, and if that's what is necessary for you to stay safe then justification is on your side.

The conflict resolution model

As a door supervisor you may experience aggressive behaviour on all levels – from verbal abuse and threats right through to potentially dangerous situations. Any decisions you make will have to be immediate and, as noted above, you may have to justify your actions. Indeed, the safety of your colleagues and members of the general public, as well as your own, may depend on the action you take in such situations – this is particularly the case when dealing with the issue of use of force. You will have to assess a situation, calculate the risks and consequences, and act swiftly. One calculation you will need to make will be in terms of the level of force you should use. This will be dictated by the level of threat directed at you, your colleagues or a third party.

To work out the level of force required in various situations, law enforcement personnel in the United States use something called the 'level of force continuum'. The police in this country have a similar thing, called the 'conflict resolution model' (see Table 2.1). It was designed to present a set of guidelines that indicate the level of force that should be used in certain situations; it may also prove useful in terms of helping you justify your actions after the event.

	Table 2.1 The conflict resolution model	
Behaviour	Impacting factors	Response
COMPLIANCE (no resistance)	Sex, age, size, strength	Door supervisor presence (observing, passive control)
VERBAL RESISTANCE (refusing to cooperate, abusive)	Skills/knowledge	Tactical communication (verbal and non-verbal)
PASSIVE RESISTANCE (refusing to move or leave)	Alcohol, drugs, mental condition	Subject control (low level of force)
ACTIVE RESISTANCE (pulling/pushing or struggling)	Injury/exhaustion, disadvantage	Subject control (increase in level of force/control restraint)
ASSAULT/AGGRESSIVE RESISTANCE (fighting, punching, kicking)	Multiple assailants, weapons danger	Defensive tactics (methods of fending, strikes/takedowns)
SERIOUS/LIFE-THREATENING RESISTANCE (armed or serious attack, risk of serious harm or death)	Serious, imminent danger to life	Serious or deadly use of force (pre-emptive strikes, action likely to cause serious harm or even death)

2.3 The law and self-defence

As we have seen, the law states that you may use 'reasonable force' to defend yourself. However, what constitutes reasonable force and under what circumstances you may use it are open to discussion and may have to be decided by the courts. The following guidelines aim to give you more of an idea of what is and is not acceptable.

- If attacked you have every right to use reasonable force to defend yourself against an unlawful attack.
- You are equally entitled to use reasonable force to prevent an unlawful attack upon yourself, your family or your property.
- Under the Criminal Act 1967 you can use reasonable force to prevent an unlawful attack upon anyone.
- In court, the claim of self-defence is proved if the defendant genuinely believed he/she was being attacked, or was in imminent danger of attack, and the response was proportionate to the perceived threat.
- If you are attacked, the courts will not expect you to calculate an exact amount of reasonable force.
- If you perceive you are threatened, you are entitled to act in self-defence and not be penalised by the courts. The law says: 'If the defendant makes a genuine mistake about

the existence of a threat, they are entitled to rely on self-defence as a defence even if no threat actually existed.'

- In law you do not have to wait for the first blow: 'A defendant need not wait until they are struck before using force in their defence.' The Court of Appeal has ruled that 'A defendant is entitled to use self-defence by striking their assailant *before* they are struck; and in exceptional circumstances, arm themselves against an expected imminent attack.'

- Although you are expected to show reasonable restraint, as a matter of law you are not obliged to retreat or show unwillingness to fight.

- The law does not give a person the 'go-ahead' to beat someone up: 'A defendant's actions must be proportionate to the perceived threat.'

- If the attack were a murderous one, then the defendant would be entitled to use extreme violence.

- If a defendant is under attack and reaches for the first available object that comes to hand, the use of that object is likely to be deemed as reasonable. Everyday items such as pens, keys, rolled-up magazines and so on, can be used against an attacker.

- You cannot by law carry anything that could be described as an offensive weapon.

Giving a statement

After an incident the police may need to take statements. These may be used as evidence in a court of law. When you make a statement you should sign every page and make the following declaration:

> This statement, consisting of [however many] pages signed by [your name], is true to the best of my knowledge and belief, and I make it knowing that, if it is tendered in evidence, I shall be liable to prosecution if I wilfully stated anything which I know to be false or do not believe to be true.

Whenever you make a statement, you must say only things that you know to be true. Giving false information or saying anything that is simply untrue is a serious offence.

Figure 2.1 After an incident, you may need to make a statement to the police

Making a statement on the use of force

When making a statement about your use of force you should record the following points:

- how you were called to the incident
- the type of incident
- who you were with – for example, was another door supervisor with you?
- what you saw, did or said

- what others did or said
- who was involved in the incident – how many people, what their attitude was
- how you approached the incident
- details of any weapons involved
- details of your decision to use force
- how much force you used – according to the person's level of resistance
- how you restrained or evicted the person
- how the person was detained until the police arrived
- details of any injuries, to you or to others
- details of the officer who took custody of the person.

Describing an incident involving a person

You may need to describe an incident in which you were not directly involved. This may mean having to describe another person. Your description needs to be precise and accurate. You should include details of the following:

- the person's physical appearance
- for how long you watched the person
- how far away the person was
- the lighting conditions – could you see clearly?
- whether you had seen this person before – and, if so, how many times
- whether there was a special reason for remembering this person.

Identifying a person to the police

When identifying a person to the police, you should note how long it was between seeing the person and your identification of them to the police, and whether their appearance had changed in any way since your first sighting of them.

A to H profile recognition

The following model offers a useful way of jogging your memory when you are giving a visual description of an individual.

- A = Age
- B = Build
- C = Colour
- D = Distinguishing features
- E = Elevation (height)
- F = Facial hair
- G = Gait
- H = Hair

2.4 Admission policy, ID checks and refusing entry

Photographic identification may be required for entry.

If you are required to provide id, please be aware that due to an increasing market in fake id, only passports and photographic driving licences will be accepted.

Figure 2.2 Sticking to an admissions policy can help to stop trouble before it starts

Refusal of entry and admissions policies

Controlling entry by refusal, and when necessary rejection, is all part of your duty as a door supervisor. Reasons for refusal may vary; any of the following would be considered a good enough reason for refusal:

- the venue is full to capacity
- a person is under the influence of alcohol or drugs
- a person is underage
- a person refuses to be searched
- a person is a known troublemaker and/or has previously been barred
- a person does not comply with the venue's dress code
- a person is found in the possession of an offensive weapon or an illegal substance
- a person cannot/will not pay the venue's entrance fee.

Remember, on no account can refusal of entry be based on race, gender or sexuality (see also Section 2.8). Discrimination is against the law. In all cases of refusing entry always strive to be polite and fully explain your reason for refusal. In circumstances such as the venue being full, explain that this is the reason – remember, you are not personally evicting this person.

Some venues adopt a one-in, one-out policy, so if the venue is currently full you can ask the individual to wait. Never forget that one of your overall objectives is to provide customer care for your clientele; this will be demonstrated when meeting and greeting your customers, and will include helping customers, dealing with their concerns and complaints, as well as controlling the door and behaviour inside the venue.

These matters are very important aspects of door work: they assist in, first, controlling the door to screen out the undesirable minority that you will undoubtedly encounter and, second, dealing with any trouble that may occur inside your venue. The first of these requires the ability to assess and weigh up certain individuals at a glance.

It is your job to control who is let in to your venue; this includes not letting in anyone who is, say, visibly drunk or under the influence of drugs, anyone who does not meet the venue's dress-code criteria, or anyone who has a history of violent or criminal behaviour. This is where trusting your instincts and having a good memory for faces can pay great dividends. When you're on the door, you have maybe the width of the pavement or the time it takes for someone to climb out of a taxi to size them up and decide whether or not they are a desirable customer or a potential troublemaker. Things to look out for are how they're dressed, whether they can walk in a straight line or appear intoxicated. Is it a lad on his own or out with his girlfriend? Or has he just walked up the road with ten of his mates only to split up into separate units so they can all gain entry to your venue?

The ideal is to keep out, or prevent from regaining admittance, those who just don't feel right, have already been refused entry, or have previously been barred or evicted from the premises. It makes more sense to contain a potential problem at the door than to have to deal with it inside. (If trouble does break out inside, the door supervisor must be prepared to deal with everything from a report of a stolen purse to a full-scale bar brawl.) At the door, you are basically a filter system, put in place to keep out any undesirable element.

Of course, it's likely that an individual will refuse to accept the reasons you give them for rejection or refusal of entry. In such cases, the guidelines laid down by the SIA suggest that, in deciding what to do about this, you refer to the policy of your venue, so you must know what this is.

In general, policies suggest that, in cases like these, you call the manager or licensee; if the person denied entry still refuses to comply after that, then the police should be called. If a person tries to enter the premises regardless, then he/she is considered to have committed the civil offence of trespass and, again, the police should be called.

As most serving door supervisors will tell you, this is where a lot of situations have the potential to turn violent, and they may do so very quickly – and probably before the police arrive. In such cases you, as door supervisor, may be required to deal with any violence and physical confrontation that may be provoked. As I mentioned in the Introduction, that's where this book comes in: it aims to help you deal with real-world situations just like this,

THE LAW IN RELATION TO DOOR SUPERVISORS

and it's something that we'll look at in detail when we come to Part Two of this book, which deals with conflict management.

Eviction

It is assumed that your venue will have its own detailed rules on how and from which exit you should evict someone. The general procedure suggested by our industry's governing body, the SIA, offers the following advice.

- Warn the person and ask them to stop the offending behaviour; tell them they will be evicted unless they stop.
- If they continue, ask them to leave and encourage them to leave of their own accord.
- If they refuse to leave, or threaten you, then you are entitled to remove them physically with reasonable and necessary force via the nearest exit.

You must use only such force as is necessary and deemed reasonable to the circumstances in order to avoid possible injury to yourself, the customer and possible damage to property. Always tell your colleagues before you take action in case you need assistance or a witness. The door supervisor has a legal duty, acting on behalf of the licensee, not to permit drunken, violent, quarrelsome or disorderly conduct on licensed premises.

If a person refuses to leave and you find it necessary to call the police, they have a legal duty to attend. One thing to consider, however, is that if calling the police for assistance to violent incidents becomes too frequent an occurrence at your venue, then its licensed status may be jeopardised and it could be shut down. That is why it is important to have a good door team and situational game plans in place for dealing with potential problems before they escalate; such plans offer valuable guidance, helping door staff to work effectively in such scenarios. It is your job to monitor the behaviour of customers inside the venue, and to deal quickly and efficiently with those who threaten the safety of other customers, spoil their enjoyment or in any way jeopardise the management's licence.

2.5 Search procedures

Figure 2.3 Appropriate search procedures play an important part in ensuring venue safety

Part of your job as a door supervisor will involve conducting search procedures on the customers that visit your venue. The need for these will depend on the kind of venue you work in and the type of event taking place. If you work in a small venue such as a public house with an entertainment licence and the majority of your customers are regulars, then you will be called upon to conduct a search less frequently than, say, if you worked in a large nightclub or the kind of venue that hosts large music and sporting events; such places make routine search procedures compulsory, and so they should be.

In the majority of cases you will need to conduct searches on customers before they enter your venue but there may also be times when you have to search someone who is already inside. It is important that you understand your venue's policy for searching customers before and after admission.

What to look out for

Customer and bag searches are carried out in order to help prevent any items being bought into the venue that may put customers or staff in danger, such as any kind of offensive weapon (by design or improvised) or any illegal item such as drugs.

These are the two main things that you should be looking out for, but you should also be on the lookout for any kind of spray or irritant, as well as bottles or containers of alcohol that might have been brought in. (The latter is a common ploy among young people and students at music gigs or events like student balls.) In my time as a doorman, I've worked at a variety of venues – from public houses, nightclubs and casinos, to boat parties, field events and large arena shows – and conducted hundreds of searches. One thing I've learnt (which is not set in stone although there is a common thread) is that where music events are concerned, and in particular dance music events, the different types of music are likely to attract different types of customer. For example, most house/trance-type music will in most cases attract a very friendly and mellow kind of crowd; this is in contrast to the drum-and-bass kind of sound, with its more aggressive beat, which will, in my experience, attract the kind of crowd that will make search procedures more necessary. It's a fact that I have found more weapons and illegal drugs at such events than I have at music events of a different kind.

However, this is just a personal observation and, of course, you are likely to find evidence to contradict it whatever the type of venue you work in. In short, with experience you will come to know which procedures should be brought into play when. This decision will also be based on the search policy laid down by the management of your venue, which may require the searching of: everyone who enters the venue; customers selected at random (for example, every fifth person), making sure that selection is not discriminatory on the grounds of colour, race, sex or disability; customers about whom you already have information or knowledge that gives cause for concern.

Conducting a search

Before any search can take place you must first ask the permission of the person who is to be searched. It is a good idea to display a notice in a prominent place, indicating that search procedures are in place so that your customers are informed and aware of this as they enter your venue. You can then tell a customer if a search is necessary and ask them if they are willing to comply; if they are not, you have the right to refuse them admission and should do so.

BE AWARE

Only female door supervisors are allowed (pending given permission) to search another female. The same rule applies to men searching men. In all cases, make sure that a witness is present.

Any standard search should follow these guidelines:

- be polite and tactful
- use professional conduct
- get permission to search
- where the eyes can't see, the hands don't go
- when searching a bag, ask the owner to remove the contents for you to see – do not touch the contents of the bag
- when searching an individual, ask them first to empty the contents of their pockets onto a table and then ask them if they have any sharp objects or needles/syringes on their person
- do not put your hands inside pockets – ask for them to be turned out
- where necessary, wear gloves to protect your hands – always take care to avoid cross-contamination from blood
- use questions to establish what the individual might be carrying.

A step-by-step guide to searching

When conducting a search and working through the points listed above, use the following method. (The method given here is for searching a conventionally dressed male; it will of course need to be adapted according to the person you are searching – a conventionally dressed female, say, or someone in costume, or particular religious or ceremonial dress.)

1. Stand slightly side on to the customer, making sure that they keep their hands out to their sides and away from their pockets. Maintain a balanced position with one foot in front of the other, equal weight on each foot.
2. Working from the top down, start with the head. If the customer is wearing a hat or headdress of some kind, ask them to remove it. Certain religions may be against the removal of a headdress; if that is the case, you will need to make a judgement call and either let it go, refuse admission or refer the matter to your senior door person. (Just as a note from real experience, I have found edged weapons concealed in such headgear on several occasions and, in one case, a fair amount of an illegal substance in the hollow of a person's dreadlock, so it does happen.)
3. From here, move on to the collar with both hands and feel from the middle outward to both ends. Then continue the movement outward, feeling the shoulders and the tops of both arms, then underneath both arms to the trunk area. Using one movement, frisk the sides of the trunk and then take your hands straight up and down the back and then the front, over the top of the upper garments to search the body.
4. Frisk over the top of all pockets, including coat and trousers; if necessary ask the customer to empty their pockets out onto a table. Remember: where the eyes can't see

the hands don't go – this is for your own protection from sharps (needles). Next, ask the person to turn around with their back to you and, in one tactful movement, squat down into a balanced crouch and feel over the top of each trouser leg in one motion from top to bottom.

5. If you feel the need, ask the person to remove their shoes as these are often used as a place of concealment.

This would be as full a search as you are allowed to conduct and you will need to use your own judgement in terms of the degree to which you stick to the above steps. Of course, if you work at a large venue and a lot of people are coming in, then searching every single one of them in this way will be time-consuming and a strain on manpower. Again, that's where judgement comes in (always adhering to venue policy, of course).

2.6 Making an arrest

There may come a time during your duty as a door supervisor when you will come across evidence of or become a witness to an offence that will require a person to be detained until the arrival of the police. In such a situation you have the same powers of arrest as any member of the public when it comes to apprehending suspects for a variety of offences.

Arrestable offences

The powers of arrest available to a door supervisor are provided under both common law and statute law (see Section 2.1). Most of the powers of arrest that door supervisors will use can be found under statute law, within the Police and Criminal Evidence Act 1984. Section 24.4 of this Act provides that 'any person may arrest, without warrant, anyone whom he has reasonable grounds for suspecting to be committing [an arrestable] offence'. Section 24.5 of the Act provides that, where an arrestable offence has been committed, any person may arrest without warrant anyone who is guilty of the offence or anyone whom s/he has reasonable grounds for suspecting to be guilty of it.

An arrestable offence might include an offence for which the sentence is fixed by law or an offence for which a person aged 21 years or over (not previously convicted) may be sentenced to imprisonment for a term of five years or more, or a specified offence not included in the previous two paragraphs, such as possession of an offensive weapon. The power of arrest without warrant also covers those attempting to commit such an offence, conspiracy to commit such an offence, or inciting, aiding, abetting or procuring any such offence. Offences under this section, for which door supervisors have the same powers of arrest as the public, include:

- murder
- rape
- ABH/GBH
- indecent assault
- firearms offences
- drug offences

- possession of an offensive weapon
- robbery
- theft
- burglary
- deception
- criminal damage.

PROCEDURE FOR MAKING A CITIZEN'S ARREST

- Use the minimum force possible to restrain the person.
- Tell them that they must wait for the police to arrive.
- Call the police immediately.
- Identify yourself as a door supervisor.
- Tell them why they must wait.
- Don't use any type of handcuffs, cable ties, string etc. to restrain them; it is illegal.
- Don't read them their rights or caution them; you are not a police officer.
- Search them *only if they give their consent*.
- Make sure you have witnesses.
- When the police arrive, tell them *in front of the suspect* what happened.

Having made an arrest, the person being detained and their welfare are your responsibility. Make sure that they are in a place of safe custody until the police arrive. You must not lose sight of the person, nor should they be left alone at any time. Be alert to any attempt by the suspect to discard evidence. Requests to use the toilet should be treated with caution, especially in cases of theft or drug-related incidents.

BE AWARE

In Hampshire they are talking about issuing door supervisors with stiff cuffs in order to restrain non-compliant individuals more effectively. This measure is also being considered for event stewards at certain football grounds. If such a thing is made commonplace then training will have to be offered. Just something to bear in mind for the future ...

2.7 Licensing law

In England and Wales, venues with door supervisors require licences to operate, which are granted by the authorities. There are two types of licence that you as a door supervisor will need to have an understanding of: the Premises Licence and the Temporary Event Notice (TEN). As a door supervisor it is your duty to know the start and finish times of the licence. Any deviation from the times within which your venue is licensed to sell alcohol or offer entertainment may result in the licence in question being suspended or revoked.

The Premises Licence

The Premises Licence covers the sale of alcohol, the late-night sale of hot food and the provision of public music, dancing and similar entertainment. There are no standard hours: some venues are licensed to sell alcohol 24 hours a day, but most are not.

The licence is granted by the local council once certain conditions have been met. Initially, technical regulations must be met, relating to the building's structure and safety as a venue for public entertainment. The police and people who live and work near the venue are also given a chance to comment on the licence application. A licence will be granted only after such an inspection has taken place and all regulations have been satisfied.

Any entertainment taking place at your venue must finish by the time specified on the licence.

The Temporary Event Notice

The TEN can be used to authorise the sale of alcohol and/or the provision of public entertainment at a specific one-off event. The event may last up to 96 hours and up to 499 people may attend.

The TEN should be kept at the venue during the event.

The fire certificate

In addition to the two main licences described above, it is also compulsory for a venue to hold a fire certificate. The main purpose of a fire certificate is to ensure that all fire safety conditions have been met and that safe evacuation is possible in an emergency. It also states the maximum number of people, including customers and staff, that can be allowed in the venue at any one time. (This is also one of the main conditions of the PEL, which likewise specifies a maximum number of people.)

If, at any time, more than the maximum number of people are present, then the licensee and any member of the management could be imprisoned for up to six months and fined up to £20,000. In addition, the venue could eventually be closed and all licences revoked.

What licensing means for you

The licensee is the person to whom a licence is granted; you should know who is the licensee of your venue. There are rules that your licensee must obey in order to be allowed to carry on a licensed business. If these rules are broken (as noted above) their licences might be revoked and the venue could be closed down, which in an obvious sense will affect everyone's job in the venue, including yours.

A major part of your job as a door supervisor is to help protect the venue's licences by striving to ensure that certain rules of conduct are kept in place and that laws in relation to licensing remain unbroken. Part of your job will require a working knowledge of licensing laws and how they relate to the public; you might need to draw upon this knowledge to state, for example:

- the law in relation to refusing entry and evicting customers
- the different types of licences and permissions available for premises
- police powers in relation to licensed premises
- the rights and duties of the licensees, and door supervisors as their representatives
- the law in relation to young persons
- the law in relation to drunkenness, disorderly conduct, prostitutes and unlawful gaming.

Proof of age/ID checks

The law strictly controls the sale of alcohol to any person(s) under the age of 18. The licensee and any person involved in the sale of alcohol to an underage person can be prosecuted.

Whenever you have any doubt about how old someone is, you should check their proof of age. Proof of age cards are not a reliable source of ID, however, as they may be fake (such things are easily bought on the internet these days). You will have to use your own judgement when checking ID. The following are the most reliable sources of identification:

- passport
- driving licence with photograph.

A person refused admission on the grounds of age alone has no legal claim against you or the venue. As noted above, the licensee can be prosecuted and the venue's licences revoked if the rules relating to young people are not followed, so you really can't be too careful.

Figure 2.4 Passports and driving licences (with photos) are the most reliable forms of ID

2.8 Equal opportunities

The door supervisor and the licensee both have the right to refuse entry and, under certain circumstances, to evict people from their premises; this is based on the law and certain rules of conduct that are in place to ensure customer safety and enjoyment. However, discrimination of any kind on the grounds of race, sex or disability is illegal.

As a licensee, or a door supervisor acting on behalf of a licensee, you cannot refuse or evict anyone on the grounds of sex, colour, race, physical appearance (for example, facial disfigurement) or disability. Refusal of entry purely on the grounds of discrimination is an offence and may lead to prosecution under the:

- Race Relations Act
- Sex Discrimination Act
- Disability Discrimination Act.

Penalties for such acts of discrimination include heavy fines and compensation claims. As a door supervisor you need to adopt a non-judgemental attitude and resist making assumptions about people based on the way they look or where they might come from. Strive to treat all your customers equally and fairly.

That said, if you are justified in your reason to refuse entry or in evicting someone from your venue based on undesirable behaviour then you must do your duty regardless of who that individual might be. Just bear in mind that making such decisions based on personal prejudice is an antiquated attitude and has no place in the field of modern door work.

CHAPTER THREE

HEALTH AND SAFETY ISSUES

3.1 Health and safety at work

Although this is a very dry subject it is necessary nonetheless, so the essentials of health and safety matters will be covered here, as set out in the handbook that accompanies the Level 2 National Certificate for Door Supervisors.

Where a workplace has five or more employees, the employer must have a written health and safety policy. This must state how duties of care (see below) will be carried out. An appropriate health and safety policy must be displayed on the premises.

Safety in the workplace

Your work premises must be safe for both customers and staff – it's the law. The safety of customers is primarily the responsibility of the licensee of the venue, but all members of staff have a 'duty of care'.

The duty of care

Where you work, everyone has a duty of care to you, and you to them. This means that:

- your colleagues have a duty of care to you
- your employer has a duty of care to staff, clients and customers.

You have to be careful that you protect yourself and others from risks to health and safety at work. You should look out for things that could cause accidents, like tripping hazards or broken glass.

If you are employed by an agency or are self-employed, the same duty of care applies.

The risk assessment

Your employer must carry out a risk assessment. This means that anything that could cause an accident will be listed. The risk assessment will:

- identify the hazards in your venue
- state how risks to the staff can be reduced.

The accident book

Details of all accidents on work premises, including those in which customers or clients are involved, must be recorded in an accident book (see Figure 3.1). You should find out where this is kept. (This is used in addition to the security incident log book.) Details of any accidents – namely the person(s) involved, the time, date and circumstances – should be entered in the book as soon as possible after they have occurred.

```
┌─────────────────────────────────────────────────────────────┐
│                    ACCIDENT REPORT FORM                      │
├───────────────────────────────┬─────────────────────────────┤
│ DATE              TIME         │ PLACE INCIDENT OCCURRED     │
│                                │                             │
├───────────────────────────────┼─────────────────────────────┤
│ NAME OF INJURED PERSON         │ ADDRESS                     │
│                                │                             │
├───────────────────────────────┤            TEL. NO.         │
│ POSITION (IF STAFF)            │                             │
├───────────────────────────────┴─────────────────────────────┤
│ DESCRIPTION OF INCIDENT:                                     │
│                                                              │
│                                                              │
├──────────────────────────────────────────────────────────────┤
│ DETAILS OF INJURY AND FIRST AID GIVEN:                       │
│                                                              │
│                                                              │
├───────────────────────────────┬──────────────────────────────┤
│ SIGNATURE OF                   │ SIGNATURE OF PERSON          │
│ INJURED PERSON .........       │ ATTENDING INCIDENT .......   │
└───────────────────────────────┴──────────────────────────────┘
```

Figure 3.1 An accident book

Reporting injuries

Injuries to employees and members of the public that occur on work premises must be reported by the employer to the local authority when, as a result of an injury:

- an employee is away from work for more than three days
- an employee or customer is taken to hospital.

Your responsibilities

The responsibility for making sure that customers and staff are safe is the licensee's, but as a door supervisor you may be required to assist in some duties.

If, as a door supervisor, you take on duties in relation to the Public Entertainment Licence (PEL) in your venue, or to health and safety regulations, then you take on the legal responsibility in addition to the licensee. For example, if, as part of your job, you agree to unlock the fire exits in your venue but do not carry this out, then both you and the licensee could be prosecuted.

The health and safety officer or the management in your workplace will tell you about any special responsibilities you may have. However, the following guidelines will help you to maintain health and safety on a day-to-day basis.

- **Know how to report hazards:** you should find out how to report hazards, dangerous incidents and injuries in your venue.
- **Keep mentally and physically fit:** your job may expose you to particular risks if you have to refuse entry or remove someone from the premises; with this in mind, you should keep mentally alert and physically fit so that you can deal with such situations.
- **Personal injury and third-party insurance:** you should be covered by adequate personal injury and third-party insurance. If your employer is a limited company they are legally bound to insure you, otherwise you will need to insure yourself.
- **Take care when lifting heavy goods:** your employer's risk assessment may identify 'manual lifting' as a risk. In order to protect yourself from injury you should follow any training or guidelines your employer gives you (see also the accompanying 'Be aware' box).
- **Take precautions against infectious diseases:** you should be very careful when handling drugs litter and blood or other spills, and also when searching people (see the information about drugs litter on page 29 of Section 3.2).
- **Tripping hazards and spillages:** tripping hazards and liquid spills are an obvious hazard – to you and the public. This is particularly the case when you are moving quickly to a scene or when escorting somebody off the premises. Be observant of your environment whenever you escort someone out. It's no use making an effective restraint on a combative subject if you then take a step back and fall over a chair or table. The same applies when dealing with an incident on the dancefloor or in the toilets. Beer, drink, water and suchlike present real and present danger of slippage, so be vigilant.

BE AWARE

Always take care when lifting anything from the floor. If an item is too heavy or beyond your capabilities then don't attempt to lift it. Alternatively get some help and, in all cases when lifting from the floor, always employ as flat a back as you can and bend both of your knees. This will allow you to lift the load equally with your legs and back in unison. Also consider using a lifting support or belt if such a duty is frequent within your field of work.

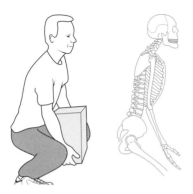  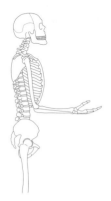

Figure 3.2 How to lift safely

First aid

It is now compulsory in any workplace for there to be on hand at least two registered persons proficient in first aid. I would suggest that, both as a door supervisor and as an individual, you seek out such training for yourself. At the very least ensure that you know where your workplace's first-aid kit is kept and familiarise yourself with the basics of ABC: airway, breathing and circulation. You should also know how to place someone in the recovery position, and how to stop or slow the flow of bleeding by using elevation and compression. Note that all accidents or incidents of injury where first aid is required are to be logged in the workplace's accident book (see page 25).

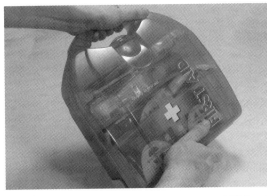

Figure 3.3 Where is your workplace's first-aid kit kept?

3.2 Drugs awareness

Drugs and licensed premises

There is absolutely no doubt that you will come across drugs and illegal substances. The main problems relating to drugs on licensed premises are drug taking, drug dealing and the deliberate spiking of drinks. It is also probable that, wherever you find such illegal activity taking place, other incidents of crime may also present themselves. Illegal drug use attracts crime – it's a fact of life. For example, drug addiction leads people into other crimes in order to get money to buy drugs, and drug dealers may engage in criminal acts against each other to get buyers. This is obviously not the kind of thing you want going on in your venue.

The most common drugs that you are likely to come across within the pub and nightclub environment are class A stimulants (see below) such as ecstasy, speed, cocaine and crack cocaine, along with the various forms of cannabis resin and weed (or skunk). Such drugs are common to the recreational user on a night out, as well as to the drug dealer who will seek the opportunity to peddle his wares beneath the neon.

During the time I worked on the doors and also within the field of close protection within the music industry, I observed certain links between drugs and music. For example, ecstasy (known on the street as Es or pills) was most often associated with dance nights, or house and boat parties that play what's known as hard house, trance and techno-style music. Someone who has taken this drug will appear excited and happy, and will commonly be referred to as 'loved up' – wanting to be friends with everyone. This person will often have a glazed, eyes-half-closed look and will not be able to keep still for long, hence the need to dance.

In contrast to this is the sound of drum and bass. As I mentioned in Section 2.5, this music has a very loud and aggressive beat and (in my experience) often attracts an array of undesirable clientele. The drugs of choice here seem to be cocaine and crack cocaine (also known as ching, Charlie or coke, and crack or rocks). This kind of stimulant is highly addictive and its users are usually quite strung out. They may appear edgy and agitated, particularly when searched. Their eyes will usually appear wide and staring, with a fair degree of dilation to the pupils. When someone who has taken crack cocaine becomes aggressive they will not listen to reason. Other effects while in an agitated state include a massive increase in strength, and they seem desensitised to pain.

Other recreational drugs common to the pub and club scene are amphetamines (also known as speed, whizz or Billy) and, of course, cannabis in its various forms, known as puff, pot, blow, weed, ganja or green, among other names. With amphetamines the user will have a fair degree of dilation to the pupils and will often talk continuously – this is often referred to as 'waffling'. The person may also bite and chew at their lips and mouth without realising that they are doing so. Other than that, there are no really obvious signs. Cannabis users will often display a very laid-back or chilled-out demeanour. The eyes are a real giveaway: they will often appear red and swollen. But the most obvious indication will be the smell of the drug as it is smoked, and the assorted drug litter left behind.

Cannabis is the most commonly found drug. A huge array of the general public, from all walks of life, smoke cannabis; and there is a fair chance that during any routine search on the door you will find some evidence of its use.

Laws relating to drugs

The Misuse of Drugs Act 1971

There are a number of laws affecting the possession, supply and trafficking of illegal drugs. The most important is the Misuse of Drugs Act 1971. This lists those drugs that are 'controlled', and gives details of the range of offences and penalties UK courts can apply in respect of each.

Public Entertainment Licence (Drugs Misuse) Act 1997

This is another important law. It gives local licensing authorities, police and the courts power to deal with the use of controlled drugs in or near places of public entertainment.

The classification of drugs

Below is a list of the principle drugs in circulation. They are split into three categories, or classes – class A, B and C – according to their potential harmfulness. The class into which a drug falls also determines the penalties for offences under the above acts. Class A drugs have the highest penalties.

- **Class A drugs:** opium, morphine, heroin, cocaine, crack, ecstasy; plus LSD, amphetamine and magic mushrooms if prepared for use.
- **Class B drugs:** amphetamines.
- **Class C drugs:** cannabis resin and weed, tranquillisers such as temazepam and flunitrazepam (also known as rohypnol, the so-called 'date rape drug'); possession of these drugs is illegal without a prescription.

Another illegal substance that has made frequent press is GHB (gamma-hydroxybutyrate), a colourless liquid sold in small bottles or capsules which are then swallowed, causing a similar effect to rohypnol. GHB may cause sedation, nausea, vomiting, confusion and memory loss. It can be lethal if mixed with other substances, particularly alcohol.

Drug-related offences

You are not expected to have detailed knowledge of the different types and classes of drugs, but the following should give you an idea of the most common drug-related offences.

- **Unlawful possession of a controlled substance:** this is when a controlled drug is found in the possession and control of a person.
- **Unlawful possession with intent to supply:** this is where a person has been found in possession of a large amount of a drug (too large to be described as for 'personal use'). Someone found in your venue with a quantity of tablets or a number of individual wraps of a drug would be liable to prosecution for this offence.
- **Supplying a controlled drug:** supplying means any of the following – selling, giving or sharing, or offering to supply a controlled drug, or being concerned in the supply of a controlled drug.

How to spot signs of drug dealing

There are several signs that might indicate that drug dealing is taking place in your venue:

- a person or group of people being very popular
- regular trips to the toilets/garden or car park area
- customers staying for a short time and not buying drinks
- deal lists – discarded pieces of paper listing numbers and names (preserve these as evidence; see Section 3.3)
- secretive or sly conduct
- information from other staff or customers
- known users/dealers frequenting premises
- money changing hands.

If drugs are found on anyone's person they should be confiscated and the police called immediately. You may have to arrest the person (see Section 2.6). Ensure that you preserve any evidence of drug litter (see Section 3.3).

While on the subject of drug litter, the most obvious danger to you as a door supervisor will be from sharps. Certain drug users will employ the use of needles when taking various drugs – for example, heroin. The obvious danger here is cross-contamination from infected blood and the risk of contracting HIV or hepatitis. It therefore bears repeating yet again: during search procedures, *'Where the eyes can't see, the hands don't go.'* Always ask a person if they are carrying anything sharp, and be aware that a drug user has the ability to employ an item such as a needle or syringe as an improvised weapon.

Figure 3.4 Drug use in the pub and nightclub environment is a fact of life

Taking action

If you suspect that someone is dealing drugs on the premises, you should observe the following guidelines.

- Inform the manager/licensee.
- Act within your venue's policy on drugs at all times (make sure that you know what it says).
- Ask other staff for help so that you have a witness and proof.
- Ask for the person's permission before you attempt to search.
- If permission to search is refused, evict the person and call the police immediately.
- If permission is given, you may search the person in accordance with the procedure outlined in Section 2.5.
- If you find what you now suspect may be drugs as a result of the search, confiscate the substances and call the police immediately.
- You may have to arrest the person (see Section 2.6).
- Check CCTV footage, if available, for evidence.

WHAT TO DO IF SOMEONE IS SUFFERING FROM THE EFFECTS OF DRUG USE

Speak calmly and reassure the person.
If possible, take them to a cooler, quieter area of the venue.
Ask their friends for their cooperation.
Find out what drugs have been taken.
Inform the management, who will decide if it is necessary to call a first-aider or the emergency services.

Never:

- put drugs in your own pocket
- take any controlled substance outside the premises
- ignore drug taking
- let anyone into your premises if you know or suspect they are drug dealers
- act on your own in a situation involving drugs – always have a witness present.

3.3 Crime scene preservation

Examples of evidence

Following a crime it can be very important for the police to obtain evidence in order to be able to convict criminals. The first rule of evidence is that 'real evidence' is best. As an example, the bottle used in an assault, or a written or oral witness account of the incident would be considered real evidence. The next best thing would be secondary evidence; an example of this would be a video recording of the incident from CCTV. Certain items – such as fingerprints, hair and blood samples – may also offer forensic evidence.

Protecting a crime scene

It is vitally important to protect the scene of a crime by preventing it from being disturbed in any way. Valuable evidence can be lost in minutes. It is important that door supervisors are in position to take charge of a crime scene until the police arrive. The most important aspects of crime-scene preservation are as follows:

- Do not let evidence be contaminated – for example, by adding fingerprints or footprints.
- Prevent evidence from being destroyed – for example, by the wiping off of fingerprints or disposal of drugs.
- Prevent evidence from being removed – for example, the removal of a glass or items that might provide evidence of drug-taking.
- Prevent evidence from being moved or shifted around – for example, by tidying up.

How to fill out a security incident log book

All incidents of violence, theft or injury must be recorded in your workplace's security incident log book (see Figure 3.5). When doing this you must be sure to detail all information relevant to the incident at hand; this includes the obvious details of the situation such as time, day, date and location, along with any details of those involved, including security staff, other members of staff, members of the public and any witnesses that were present at the scene. Also make a record of whether any call was made to the emergency services (police/ambulance/fire service etc.); log who made such a call and be sure to sign and date the incident stating your position in the workplace. Remember to add as much detail as possible, as this document may need to be produced as evidence within a court of law.

Incident report *Continue on another sheet if necessary*

Date _____   Time _____

Member of staff reporting incident

Name _____   Position _____

Details of person assaulted (if appropriate)

Name _____

Position (if member of staff) _____

Address _____

Details of assailant (if known)

_____

Details of witness(es) if any

Name _____

Position (if member of staff) _____

Address _____

Details of incident

Type of incident (e.g. how was the person causing a nuisance; if assault, what injuries were suffered and what treatment received?)

_____

Location of incident (attach sketch if appropriate)

_____

Description of incident (events leading up to incident; description of assailant; if a weapon was involved)

_____

Outcome (e.g. police called, assailant evicted from premises, assailant banned)

_____

Name and contact details of police officer involved, and incident number or crime reference number, as appropriate

_____

Any other relevant information

_____

Signed _____   Dated _____

Figure 3.5 An example of a security incident log book

When the police arrive, tell them what you have seen and done. A full and accurate account of the incident should be logged as soon as possible after it happened. All notes in the log book should show the time and date they were written and should be counter-signed by a witness. Any members of staff involved should make their own notes regarding the incident. Such practice will help you if you ever have to make a statement to the police or give evidence in court. As well as the log book, it is also advisable to record details of any personal involvement in incidents in your own personal notebook. Use this only for work-related reports in case you need to produce it as evidence in court yourself.

CHAPTER FOUR

WHAT TO DO IN AN EMERGENCY

4.1 Dealing with emergencies

Door supervisors will need to be prepared for any and all kinds of emergency. A sound understanding of the kinds of emergency that you are most likely to face, along with good teamwork and well-practised preparation, will pay dividends when the time comes to deal with such situations.

The main reason that entertainment venues are required to have a Public Entertainment Licence is to ensure that the public are safe while on the premises. The licensee must have procedures in place for dealing with emergencies. These should be practised on a regular basis and should be known to you and all your door-security colleagues. As a door supervisor there are five main emergencies you may have to deal with:

1. fire
2. bomb alert
3. gas explosions and leaks
4. CS gas, OC spray and similar irritants
5. lighting failure.

We will now look at the first two of these in some detail. For the remaining three, please familiarise yourself with your workplace's policy on dealing with emergencies.

4.2 Fire safety

Fire is one of the greatest risks to the public in entertainment venues. It is your duty to watch out for any fire risks and report them to management.

THE 'TRIANGLE OF FIRE'

The three components of the so-called 'triangle of fire' are:

1. fuel
2. heat, and
3. oxygen.

If any one of these is not present a fire cannot start. In theory, a fire can be extinguished by removing one of these components – for example, covering the flames with a fire blanket removes oxygen.

Fire procedure

The first thing to do if you discover a fire is to raise the alarm immediately. Each member of staff must ensure that they know how the alarm system works in your venue in case they are the first person to find the fire. All venues must have their own type of fire alarm and methods of raising that alarm. It is your responsibility to know:

- where the alarm is located
- how the alarm works
- how to raise the alarm
- what the alarm sounds like.

Figure 4.1 Know where your venue's fire exits are and how to raise the alarm

You must also know the correct procedure for calling the emergency services. You need to know who is responsible for this, as well as how to call them yourself if the person usually responsible for this duty is not available. A door supervisor must not induce panic by shouting 'FIRE!' or indicate to the public that a fire has broken out, as this could lead to mass panic and loss of control.

WARNING

Unless you are a trained fire-fighter, you should not tackle a fire yourself. You could put yourself at risk and cause the fire to spread more quickly.

What to do once the alarm has been raised

Once the alarm has been raised you should immediately start to put in place your workplace's procedures for evacuating the premises. Each and every licensed premises should have a designated evacuation procedure in place for use during emergencies and it is your responsibility to know exactly how this works.

The procedure should have instructions for use in all types of emergency situation that might affect the safety of customers and staff. It should offer clear guidelines and specify all steps to be taken in such emergencies and by whom. All customers and staff should be clearly directed to a designated evacuation meet-up safety point outside the building.

Customers evacuating the premises via the designated fire exits should be advised to stay calm and follow instructions, and instructed to walk and not run. They should be evacuated via the nearest and safest route available, and door supervisors should give assistance to anyone who requires it – *without putting themselves at risk.*

As each part of the building is completely cleared and emptied of people you should (if possible) close all doors and windows to prevent the spread of fire. You should never ignore a fire alarm just because you think it might be a false alarm – always find out for sure.

Colour of stripe		Contents	Use
Red	 WATER	Water	Unsafe all voltages. Wood, paper, textiles, etc.
Blue	 POWDER	Dry powder	Safe all voltages. Flammable liquids.
Cream	 FOAM	Foam	Unsafe all voltages. Flammable liquids.
Black	 CO2	Carbon dioxide (CO_2)	Safe all voltages. Flammable liquids.
Green	 WET CHEMICAL	Vapourising liquids	Safe all voltages. Flammable liquids.

Figure 4.2 You should know the correct type of extinguisher to use, depending on the emergency

Occupancy numbers

As we have already seen (in Section 2.7), a venue's fire certificate will specify a maximum-occupancy figure. This figure details the maximum number of people – including customers and staff – that are permitted in the venue at any one time. There are a number of variables that will affect this number, including the amount of time required to evacuate the premises in the event of fire, the distance to the exits from any point in the venue, and the number, size and positions of exits.

Based on this information, it is vitally important that door supervisors do not allow the venue to exceed the capacity stated in the occupancy figures. The local fire authority has the power to close down and bring proceedings against any venues that violate this rule.

A lot of venues will use a counter, or 'clicker', system, which allows the door supervisor to 'count in' the number of people entering (including staff) and, using a second clicker, to 'count out' the number of people who leave. This allows staff to obtain an accurate figure of the number of people left in the venue, which is of course vitally important information in such an emergency.

Door staff have several duties to perform once the fire brigade has been called and all staff and customers have been evacuated. These are as follows.

■ Wait for the fire brigade at the venue's entrance and direct them to the fire; inform them if anyone else is left inside and warn them of any potential hazards or dangers inside the premises. Answer any questions that the fire officer may ask and carry out any instructions they may give you.

- Ensure that all members of staff are present and accounted for.
- Keep customers and all members of the public away from the entrances and exits to ensure that the emergency services have clear and unobstructed access.
- Prevent people from re-entering the building until they have been told that it is safe to do so by the senior fire officer.
- Administer first aid to anyone who requires it until the arrival of ambulances, if required.

4.3 Bomb threat

Any entertainment venue that is open to the public can be considered a potential target for a terrorist bomb attack or bomb threat. For this reason, it is everybody's responsibility to remain vigilant and to be aware that such a potential threat does indeed exist. You should be on the lookout for any kind of suspect package or suspicious activity that could indicate such an event. The chances of a terrorist attack are small, but they exist nonetheless. The most important thing to do is to report any suspicious package to the management straight away.

It is the licensee's responsibility to provide a clear written procedure for dealing with bomb threats or the finding of any suspicious package or object in your premises. It is your duty as a door supervisor to be familiar with and understand this procedure for dealing with such an emergency.

The chances of a bomb threat or terrorist activity occurring at your place of work will depend on a variety of factors. If you work in a high-profile location at a popular venue that attracts large crowds then the potential risk is likely to be higher than if you work the door at a small, nondescript pub with a music licence. That said, certain terrorist organisations can, and will, carry out indiscriminate attacks on premises that attract large numbers of people who regularly use them. Managers of such venues are now legally obliged (under the Health and Safety at Work Regulations 1992) to assess the likely risks to the safety of all members of staff and customers on the premises.

Taking proactive action

The following advice will allow your door team to take preventative measures for dealing with the potential bomb-threat emergency.

- Follow stringent search procedures at the point of entry, particularly where bags and luggage items are present.
- Be on the lookout for any suspicious activity or behaviour.
- Verbally challenge anyone who is found in areas where they should not be.
- Watch out for any suspicious packages or items, and check for any abandoned articles at the end of the evening.
- Report anything suspicious to the management so that the police can be called to investigate.

Dealing with a bomb-threat phone call

If your venue has received a bomb-threat warning via a phone call, as is common in such situations (regardless of whether or not the call is a hoax), there are five points that should be noted, particularly if you are the person receiving the call.

1. Make a careful note of what is said, getting as much information as possible.
2. Note the accent or any unusual aspects of the caller's voice.
3. Note down any specified code words that may be used.
4. After hanging up, dial 1471 – it may give you the caller's number.
5. Immediately report to the management what you have just heard.

Evacuation procedure

It is the licensee's responsibility to decide whether or not to evacuate the premises in the event of a bomb scare. Whenever possible, advice from the police should be sought. In some situations evacuation could increase rather than reduce the risks. If the building *is* to be evacuated, follow the same procedure as for a fire evacuation (see page 35 in Section 4.2) unless the location of the suspect device means customers must be evacuated via a particular exit.

People should be asked to take all of their belongings with them if they are to hand and if this will not delay the evacuation – this will make it easier to search the building later.

BE AWARE

All door supervisors should strive to remain vigilant at all times, and on the lookout for any suspicious activity that might be connected with terrorism or arson. Remember that pre-entry checks and regular performance checks can identify potential problems before they become emergencies.

PART TWO
COMMUNICATION AND CONFLICT MANAGEMENT

CHAPTER FIVE

AWARENESS OF AGGRESSIVE BEHAVIOUR

5.1 Introduction

This part of the book is really its core, and the area I'm most concerned with. Although I will refer to the guidelines from current Security Industry Authority (SIA) legislation throughout – particularly when I think a relevant point is being made – I will also cover communication and conflict management from the point of view of a door supervisor who has worked in this area for some time, and present the conclusions I have come to as a result of that experience.

As I stated in the main Introduction to this book, it is *my personal view* that the information given in the 'Conflict Management' section of the SIA manual is insufficient to prepare the door supervisor with the information and skills needed to deal with the reality of the violent minority. If you work on the doors, there is little doubt that you will have to deal with physical violence.

This factor can and will endanger the safety of all concerned if not managed effectively. Any good door supervisor will *always* – without exception – strive to resolve potential conflict through non-physical actions, and that's why, in this book, I'm going to do my best to help you take this route. Good observation and people skills are vitally important, so what we are concerned with here is encouraging you to use an understanding of body language, alongside the skills of de-escalation and verbal dissuasion.

That said, there is no way that I can write a book relating to the subject of door work without addressing the physical aspects and skills necessary to counter violence. The reason that such training is not covered in the SIA's training structure is probably due to a number of reasons, the most obvious of which is the issue of litigation. It is my aim to provide the reader with the information necessary to plug this gap – and I'll do the best that my knowledge and experience will allow. Bear in mind that some of the information offered here may be controversial but, at the same time, please do try to understand that, in certain situations, the only thing that may keep you safe and allow you to deal with real aggression and violence safely and efficiently is what you can learn from individuals who have actually done the job and can speak from real experience.

The techniques presented here are in no way intended to offer a set-in-stone 'how to' method of doing things. They simply set out for the reader some tried-and-tested methods that have worked for a variety of people who have dealt with violence in the area of nightclub door work. Read and study this book with an open mind and take from it what you will.

5.2 Communication skills and conflict management

Objective (SIA)

To ensure that door supervisors have the appropriate communication skills and knowledge of conflict management.

- Discuss communication skills and conflict management
- State the importance of customer care
- State the need to calm difficult situations and avoid violence
- State what risks can occur during violence at work
- Identify the most common conflict flashpoints

(SIA definition)

Risk assessment for the role of door supervisor

The workplace must be safe – that is the law – and your employer has a legal duty to make sure that this is so. When a manager employs door supervisors he or she must consider the job role carefully and acknowledge that, sometimes, the door supervisor's job can be dangerous. According to the Health and Safety Executive, work-related violence is defined as an assault or threat that occurs while the victim is working and which is perpetrated by members of the public.

The potential risks a door supervisor may face come under three main headings – people, objects and places – and these may pose the problems listed below.

People
- Large numbers of people
- People who are drunk or under the influence of drugs
- People who are frustrated after being refused entry, being searched or being evicted
- People with a history of anger or aggression
- Known criminals

Objects
- Offensive weapons made to cause injury or items adapted to cause injury
- Any object used to cause injury
- Items such as needles, which may cause injury or infection during searches
- Blood spills, which can cause cross-infection

Places

- Routes to and from work
- Remote areas away from CCTV coverage
- Poor lighting
- Excessive noise leading to poor communication
- Stairs
- Wet and slippery floors
- Broken and discarded glass(es)

Minimising risk

In order to minimise risk, employers must employ only door supervisors who are licensed with the SIA. All SIA-licensed door supervisors will have completed training to ensure that they have the skills necessary to deal with potentially risky or conflict situations.

The importance of conflict management and being proactive in your job

You can be proactive by preparing yourself to deal with any conflict situation that may arise at your place of work. Conflict management is a problem-solving approach. The door supervisor needs to be able to recognise a situation, decide on an appropriate solution and then act.

The need to be proactive

Every incident is the end result of a series of events. The proactive door supervisor understands the signs of potential risk and conflict before they become a real threat and is able to respond in a way that will prevent a situation from escalating. A door supervisor who can do this greatly reduces the risks of their job. This benefits both the door supervisor and the venue, and ensures that its customers can enjoy a safe night out.

Preparing to be proactive

You can prepare yourself to deal with most situations by:

- taking your professional development seriously
- keeping your knowledge and training up to date
- fully understanding practice and procedure at your workplace
- ensuring equipment, such as radio and CCTV, is in good working order
- establishing clear roles and responsibilities.

Managing customer expectations

The vast majority of customers come to a venue to enjoy a good night out. Some, however, have unreasonable expectations of the service offered. For example, they may expect to get straight in to a venue without queuing, and when they find they have to queue they may become frustrated. Such a situation will worsen if their expectations are not managed properly. Conflict management is about managing this and many other 'everynight' situations.

The need to calm situations and avoid violence

Quite apart from the fact that incidents of violence are extremely unpleasant for customers, they can lead to the revocation of a venue's licence. Also, violence often results in assault and assault is, of course, against the law.

Dealing with anger and frustration

There are always certain activities, incidents or times of the day when frustration and anger are especially likely to occur. It is important to find out the main causes of frustration and flashpoints. Then you can take steps to reduce the risk of aggression.

Common conflict flashpoints

Clearly you may need to manage conflict any time and anywhere, but there are certain recognisable flashpoints. During your practical training you will practise dealing with incidents connected with some of the following:

- long and slow-moving queues
- customers being asked to be searched at any time
- customers being refused entry for a number of reasons, such as
  - the venue is full
  - the customer is drunk or under the influence of drugs
  - the customer looks underage and has no proof of age
  - the customer refuses to be searched
  - the customer has been banned
  - the customer can't or won't pay the entrance fee
  - the customer has a bad attitude (for example, is quarrelsome or swearing).

Managing unacceptable conduct inside the venue

Examples of unacceptable conduct or breaches of rules that you might have to manage include:

- dancing on tables
- taking bottles onto the dance floor (where management does not allow this)
- bringing in alcohol not purchased in the venue
- poor reaction to slow service at the bar
- disputes with bar staff (e.g. over claimed short-changing)
- breaches of licensing law
- taking away drinks at the end of drinking-up time
- not leaving the venue at closing time.

Clearly, though, there are some less common situations that are more risky than the above:

- arrest situations
- someone in possession of weapons or drugs
- fights or assaults

- theft
- criminal damage.

You can reduce the chances of conflict by developing self-awareness – that is, understanding your own reactions when you are stressed, frustrated or angry, or when confronted with a threatening situation – and recognising the importance of maintaining self-control and objectivity. We will cover all issues of relevance to this as we go on; for now I want to focus on one extremely important fundamental – particularly if we intend to remain proactive in terms of preventing problems before they escalate. To do that, we must make maximum use of our skills of observation.

5.3 Awareness and observation skills

Awareness

That you always need to be 'switched on' should go without saying, but for door work it's absolutely essential. With this in mind, some 25 years ago a combat pistol instructor called Jeff Cooper developed a system of colour 'conditions' to define varying states of awareness. These are described below.

Condition white (switched off)

This is what people working within the field of close protection and bodyguarding call 'wide asleep'. It is logical to assume that any attack on your person while you are in this state will be an ambush and will happen before you even realise that you have a problem. If such a problem occurs in your place of work – a fight, for example – it will suddenly seem to be in full swing if you have failed to notice the early signs: eye contact, raised voices etc. Had you been switched on, you would at least have been able to apply a proactive approach and may have caught the problem earlier.

Condition yellow (alert, switched on)

This is a state of alert awareness for the full scope of your peripheral vision. You are switched on to your environment, and everyone and everything within it. This is how you should strive to be at all times, right up to the point you get home after your shift.

Condition yellow alpha (active sonar)

This yellow variant was originally developed for VIP close protection by defensive tactics instructor Dennis Martin, and explains the state of heightened awareness where you are actively scanning for a threat. The difference between the two yellow conditions (see above) can be understood in terms of the way a radar works on a battleship: there is the passive sonar, which does a sweep of the surrounding area to observe anything in the region, and then there's the active sonar, which rotates at a higher speed and alerts the operator of anything that should not be there – in other words, it is actively scanning.

Condition orange (alarm bells ringing)

This occurs when a possible situation is developing around you and you need to make an assessment of the potential danger. It is the condition that sends your mind into 'guard' state. You see something that attracts your attention and immediately begin to assess and question: 'Is this a threat?'

Condition red (time for action)

This is a state when a decision for action must be taken on the spot in order to deal with a situation.

The ideal condition

Ideally, you need to be in a 'yellow' condition of awareness as a matter of course. To sum up: 'white' is for unready; 'yellow' for alert; 'orange' for alarmed and prepared; and 'red' for action. In the accompanying box there is an example that is applicable to a typical door-work scenario.

Figure 5.1 Being caught unawares could turn out to be costly

Colour conditions: an example

Two members of door staff are standing at the door of a public house. Both are within earshot of the bar inside. Both are in **condition yellow**, and switched on. Suddenly raised voices are heard at the bar; both door supervisors switch to **condition orange** in order to make a threat assessment. They arrive at the bar to see two individuals posturing aggressively to each other. Both door supervisors then strive to separate the two individuals in an effort to defuse the situation. If aggression continues or is directed at either door supervisor, they would then shift to **condition red**, ready to take whatever action is needed to end the situation immediately.

The OODA Loop

This concept was originally developed for training jet-fighter pilots in situational awareness. It too is now also very popular within the field of VIP close protection, and is known as the OODA Loop (OODA is an acronym for observation, orientation, decision and action). When you are in a state of relaxed alertness, or condition yellow, you are constantly observing (O) your environment. If you spot a potential problem, you would then orientate (O) – that is, focus your attention on whatever it is that you've observed and determine whether or not it is a threat.

At that point you make a decision (D) as to how you are going to act on this information, which then takes you into action (A), where you put into effect the result of your decision.

You act, then you go back into the loop, starting again by observing (O): you observe how the situation has changed as a result of your action. The cycle thus becomes a continuous loop of observation, orientation, decision and action.

In the accompanying box, you will find a hypothetical example of how the OODA Loop can be applied to your working game plan.

The OODA Loop: an example

You're in position, standing by the bar. You're switched on, in tune and Observing your environment. You observe two lads at the other end of the bar, who are starting to get loud and abusive to the surrounding patrons. You Orientate that they are looking for trouble with whoever happens to make eye contact with them, and are therefore a potential threat. You then Decide what you are going to do. In this example you take Action by calling for assistance. (I am assuming that all of your team members have an established communications plan and that you are all conversant with any code words or call signs you may employ.)

With the assistance of your colleague(s) you would make your presence apparent. Based on your present Observation, you decide to talk to the men in an attempt to find out the source of their agitation. It is here that you must strive to protect your own personal space (see Section 6.4, which deals with situational control) and if possible talk the situation down to a non-physical conclusion. You would then move back into Observation to see how the situation has changed and whether there is going to be a new Orientation.

If, as in this scenario, the troublemakers appear to direct their aggressive intention towards you and your colleague(s) then that will Orientate a different Decision/Action cycle, which you would then proceed with (a physical response may indeed become necessary at this point). If nothing further develops, and the individuals start to leave as requested, then you should see them out and simply carry on with further Observation of your environment.

Visual/verbal observation

Another method that is often used within the security industry is visual/verbal observation. This is basically 'saying it as you see it'. The police use this method on advanced driving courses where the driver is encouraged to state aloud his/her observations of the road ahead, including anything and everything relevant to the immediate environment. By following this practice you are completely focused on what is going on around you at that moment in time. This will automatically raise your level of awareness and enable you to spot any potential problem early, which will in turn allow you to avoid any possible escalation. Of course, it probably isn't a good idea to speak out loud as you scan your workplace environment, but you can and should 'read out' what you see, in your head.

This is the system that a friend of mine, veteran doorman Jamie O'Keefe, used to use. Before becoming a self-protection instructor and full-time writer Jamie used to work the doors of Soho in London's West End. Like many a good doorman, he quickly made use of what worked for him. Here is one such example:

All emergency exits clear, group of lads gathering by the bar area, no obvious threat, two members of security staff visible by the main entrance and toilet area, couple arguing by the dance floor, glass dropped by the fruit machine, door supervisor *en route* …

In this job it is really easy to allow yourself to drift off into thinking about trivia, such as what you need to do tomorrow or what you watched on telly last night. In other words, it is easy to switch off and start daydreaming, particularly if you are bored and starting to get tired. Sod's law dictates that it's at just such a time that something will happen, and before you know it you'll have lost sight of your surroundings and will find yourself on the back foot.

Try to stay switched on and practise actively scanning your environment for any possibility of danger. Strive to make this habitual, just as it should be when you drive your car. It may take a little practice, but such effort will pay great dividends in terms of your ability to spot a potential threat before it unfolds.

5.4 Monitoring aggressive behaviour

This section is based on SIA definitions.

The emotional vs the rational

People have two ways of dealing with a situation: the emotional (based on feeling) and the rational (based on thought). These two aspects work together, and are balanced most of the time. However, when we are particularly upset or feel threatened, the emotional quickly takes over; this means that we lose much of our ability to rationalise and think clearly.

Animals tend to respond automatically when something threatens them. If you pull a dog's tail it is very likely that it will bite you. This is the dog's automatic reaction. Humans, on the other hand, are different. They have a choice of how they respond to a threatening situation: at first emotion kicks in – our bodies prepare to fight or to run away from a situation; as our rational side catches up, we can start to analyse the situation and respond more appropriately.

A good example of this is when we are at home and think we are alone in the house. If a family member or housemate walks into the room unexpectedly, this will make us jump. It is a very sudden fright response. However, we quickly realise that there is no threat, so we choose not to fight or run away.

Additional notes on monitoring aggression

At some point or another all door supervisors will inevitably encounter aggression; when people feel like things are not quite going their way they will often start to get upset and allow emotions to take over. This may start to manifest itself in the shape of verbal and/or physical aggression. Sometimes rude, insulting or antagonistic behaviour is to be expected. Basically, it goes with the job, so you must, where possible, learn to ignore it. Instead you should try to get at the problem that is the source of the agitation and then come up with a sensible solution to resolve it.

Sometimes, however, certain individuals may exceed what is generally seen as acceptable in terms of behaviour, leading to threats of violence or actual physical assault. In such a situation the door supervisor will have to react straight away, in an attempt to defuse the situation, or resort to the use of countermeasures to control or subdue the level of violence presented.

Obviously each situation is different and will have to be assessed on the spot according to the level of threat to you and anyone else that may be involved. What is of the utmost importance is that, as an individual, you are able to control your own emotions in order to avoid escalating the situation further via any aggressive or antagonistic response on your part. Keep in mind that you are a paid professional and part of your job is to deal effectively with such behaviour. If you overreact and take each situation personally you are going to make the job harder for yourself. Understand too that, in most cases, you are simply a vent for this individual's frustration. When people get pissed off that things are not going their way all they might see is a person in black and white, wearing a badge, who represents their problem – and, rightly or wrongly, they may insult you for it. If you have any personal hot-spots that cause you to overreact, then you will find yourself being controlled by this individual via your own emotions. If you are a bit overweight and wear glasses, say, and every time someone calls you 'a four-eyed fat bastard' you come out swinging, then this line of work is not for you.

Just be happy in your own skin and remember that this is all part of the job, so handle it with superior intellect and save getting physical for those times when self-preservation really is called for. A good understanding of body language, coupled with an awareness of incidents and areas that are likely to instigate aggression in others (such as refusal of entry or asking someone to leave), should allow you to anticipate such behaviour and develop pre-planned answers to help you deal with such situations.

You will also need to learn to use tact when dealing with potentially confrontational subjects. Be polite when you tell someone that you think they have had too much to drink. If someone does not conform to your venue's dress code and you see them join the end of the queue to gain entry don't let them wait until they get to the door to refuse them; instead politely tell them straight off and save them a long and fruitless wait.

Trusting your instincts

I have always maintained that you should trust your instincts – for example, if someone just doesn't feel right when they come to your door. (I am talking about a genuine feeling about a person here, that says something troublesome is afoot, and am by no means talking about any personal like or dislike, or judgement based on the way a person may look.) Sometimes all you have is the width of the pavement as they get out of a taxi to make an assessment. In such cases, pre-planned reasons for refusal can be very useful. Cite dress code or the members-only rule, whatever … but make it polite. The kind of instinctive feeling I am talking about will only come with experience and, of course, if the individual concerned is a known troublemaker then the same applies. You should also ensure that you are familiar with the law and all of your venue's policies. Having set-answers to customer complaints and decisions they may not agree with or understand will help create justification and understanding, and will go a long way towards defusing a potentially volatile situation.

5.5 Understanding aggressive behaviour

As a situation starts to become heated, during the verbal stage of a potential confrontation, the door supervisor will need to monitor the body language and demeanour of the individual concerned, in order to latch on to any verbal or physical cue which may indicate that the situation is about to turn violent. With experience, you will start to develop a gut feeling as to when a situation is about to turn nasty.

It is important to try to gain an understanding of the kind of pre-fight indicators a potential aggressor may display as this will provide you with a little pre-warning as to what kind of action they may take. You need to learn and recognise such signals as preparation for violence in order to prepare yourself, both physically and mentally, for imminent attack.

Such cues may also provide you with enough time to call for assistance from either the rest of your door team or, if necessary, the police – although it is likely that the situation will become physical before the police arrive. Nonetheless, making such a call for assistance may even help to defuse the situation. Recognition of the initial signals of aggressive behaviour will also provide you with just enough time to assess your level-of-force options.

The kind of aggression that we as door supervisors are likely to come up against falls into two categories: verbal and physical. The first can, and often will, lead to the second: violence. For example, an argument may start between two individuals or two groups of people, at any time for any trivial reason. It usually takes the form of eye contact followed by verbal aggression, such as shouting and swearing. Then it may progress gradually to violence, or it may just 'kick off', although in most instances there is some kind of physical or verbal cue beforehand to indicate that violence is on the way. This is why awareness (being switched on) and having an understanding of body language is so essential for us as door staff, so that we may catch and defuse a potentially violent situation before it escalates.

The threat to the door supervisor

Whenever you have to intervene to stop a potential fight, or go straight in and grab hold of people to drag them out because a fight has already started, that's the point when you must expect the physical to be directed at you. In this kind of situation, door staff must work together in pairs or as a group, and must together have an effective understanding of workable physical restraint.

Another time that you may be vulnerable to aggression, both verbal and physical, is when you have to refuse entry or ask somebody to leave. It's at such times that door staff are considered fair game, at least by the trouble-making 'beer monster' types out there. Remember, wherever you get people and alcohol in the same place you have a recipe for violent aggression.

Attack rituals

There are many types of violence and aggression that can be displayed within a countless variety of situations, but those that security staff may come across within the pub/nightclub environment can be divided into three categories, as described below.

The surprise attack

If you have no awareness, then any situation you find yourself in will be a surprise attack. That is, you will be punched out before you've realised what's happening. This could also apply if someone grabbed you or hit you from behind, as you are preoccupied dealing with someone else. Staying switched on, and working in pairs or as a group will effectively reduce the chances of this.

The 'square go'

This is the pre-decided 'square go' outside in the car park, or when someone offers you outside for a one-on-one. This is not as common as it used to be, but still happens now and again. I'm sure that most doormen have been offered out during their time in the job. Of course, going outside makes the situation personal, requires bottle and must be a personal choice.

The verbal distraction

This kind of aggressor will start things off with some form of verbal dialogue (see the accompanying box on physical and verbal cues). This is usually aggressive, and will probably include some kind of distracting question such as 'Have you got a f**king problem?' Or, if you have had to intervene in someone else's argument, it may be 'What the f**k's this got to do with you?'

Beware also that some people may use deceptive dialogue such as 'Have you got a light, mate?', or any kind of question that will engage your attention. The question may be used as a distraction to occupy your thoughts for a second as the aggressor closes the gap and erupts into violence. Then it is likely that you will either be punched or head-butted in the face.

From here the aggressor will seize the initiative and keep hitting until you are knocked to the ground, whereupon you will be kicked and stamped senseless (at this point his mates will join in). The whole thing will be over in a few seconds.

Aggressive dialogue as a prelude to physical violence

The most common dialogue you are likely to come across is the aggressive kind. Whenever you intervene to stop an argument or fight, or ask someone to leave or have to refuse them entry, you are setting the scene for this kind of aggressive dialogue. In a lot of cases this behaviour will be accompanied by an attack ritual or body language such as *arm splaying*, in a fit of exclamation. This is a way of making the aggressor appear physically bigger before an attack.

You are also likely to see *neck pecking*, in the manner of a cockerel, usually in conjunction with dropping into single syllables, such as 'Yeah' and 'And'. In addition, the aggressor's eyes may bulge, due to the *tunnel vision* that accompanies an adrenalin rush, making them wide and staring. He may also *stance up*, turning himself sideways to present less of a target, in preparation for attack.

These are just some of the physical cues that may accompany aggressive dialogue. What is important to realise is that this behaviour is in fact a kind of *interview*.

The verbal aggressor will constantly analyse your body language and may change his behaviour in order to get a certain response from you. The response he is looking for is the slightest indication of fear, or any sign to show him that he has psyched you out. If he finds any such signal, this will tell him that you are a safe bet to intimidate, and will allow him to progress to the physical attack/assault.

You must bear in mind that all of this can happen very quickly, so it is vital that you project confidence and a firm self-assurance at all times. If you do not do this then it's almost certain that physical action will follow. In most cases, when you show no sign of intimidation and demonstrate that you are not worried by an aggressor, there will be a stand-off, giving you a chance to talk the situation down.

Sometimes, however, things may get physical regardless of how you act. In such cases, where you're dealing with the kind of individual who is determined to use physical force, the only way to avoid violence is to show him that you too are prepared to get as physical as the situation demands. If you look, act and remain calm in the face of such aggression, not showing any outward signs of intimidation, then this is one way of showing the person that you have seen it all before, from bigger and better, and are indeed prepared to deal with whatever comes. This can have the effect of making the aggressive individual doubt his or her own ability and abort. There are also other variables to consider: what you say will have a bearing, and the ideal is to be non-confrontational, yet firm and determined. The majority will back off saying something like 'Yeah, well, I'll see you again.' This is usually a vain attempt to redeem themselves in front of anyone who might be present.

That just leaves the small minority that will take you up on it. So always be prepared for the physical and, as mentioned above, work together in effective pairs or groups to ensure back-up.

Dealing with the experienced aggressor

The experienced aggressor may change his behaviour when he realises that you're not in the least bit intimidated. At this point he may apologise, and give you the 'no hard feelings' routine, offering you a handshake only to pull your face straight on to a head-butt or punch. This kind of subtle deceptive trap is quite common, so be wary when offered a handshake after a show of aggression. Finally, try to gain an understanding of how these individuals work – what makes them tick. This understanding will develop over time when you are actually doing the job, taking your knowledge into the field and observing human behaviour.

Pre-conflict cues and aggressive body language

Verbal cues:

- offensive and insulting language
- loud screaming and shouting (threats)
- disjointed and unintelligible speech (abnormal stuttering)
- rapid speech (high-pitched voice)
- single-syllable answers to questions (such as 'Yeah', 'So', 'And')
- abuse focused on an individual.

Figure 5.2 Physical cue 1: 'arms splayed' stance

Physical cues:

- red face from blood surge
- increased breathing
- vein protruding from face/neck (see Figure 5.3)
- clenched fists (extreme body tension)
- hunching of shoulders
- wide-eyed stare
- finger pointing (prodding)
- hand concealment (shift of body)
- chest puffed out, hands/arms splayed (see Figure 5.2)
- neck/head pecking
- finger beckoning
- close in – invading personal space
- excessive eye contact
- head and chin pushed forwards
- clenched teeth (see Figure 5.3).

Remember, the aggressor will probably only display one or two of these cues: which of them will depend on the individual. However, the appearance of any of them is a clear indication that a physical attack is imminent, which is why awareness of aggressive body language is an essential tool for the successful door supervisor.

Figure 5.3 Physical cue 2: clenched teeth and protruding neck veins

CHAPTER SIX

CONTROLLING A SITUATION

6.1 Recognising and defusing conflict

This chapter presents some of the suggested guidelines put forward by the SIA. As you will see, all of this information, regardless of its source, has the same objective in mind: to defuse potentially hostile situations, where possible without having to resort to the physical option. This is after all the ideal method that all door supervisors should seek to employ, at all times. The information from the SIA is complemented here by material from a variety of sources, including active learning gained from the real experience of people who have actually done the job of door supervisor for years.

Signalling non-aggression

The following model – known as the 'Four As' – will help you when you are dealing with conflict situations.

1. Don't get **A**ngry
2. Manage **A**buse
3. Maintain a positive **A**ttitude
4. Be **A**ssertive

Factors that display non-aggressive behaviour include:

- comfortable distance
- relaxed shoulders and facial expression
- calmer voice
- open hands
- normal eye contact
- avoidance of sudden/jerky movements.

Giving the right message through your behaviour

Understanding the difference between aggressive and non-aggressive behaviour will help you in your job. It will also help you to project the right message through your own behaviour. People usually prefer to communicate with someone who is non-threatening rather than someone who seems aggressive. Remember: behaviour affects behaviour. Non-aggressive behaviour is more likely to encourage non-aggressive behaviour.

The 'open PALMS' model

The following model, known as 'open PALMS', will help you to remember how to signal non-aggression:

- **P** = **Position** allow exit routes, don't block in
- **A** = **Attitude** display positive and helpful attitude
- **L** = **Look & listen** normal eye contact, active listening
- **M** = **Make space** maintain a comfortable distance
- **S** = **Stance** shoulders relaxed and turned away to the side.

We will now break down this model and look at each of the factors involved in more detail.

Open PALMS

An open-handed gesture is a very powerful signal that you don't want to fight. It is connected with the reason why we shake hands in greeting. (This originated from the times when people always carried weapons. When approaching someone they used to show an extended open right palm to prove they were not threatening the other person with a weapon. This slowly developed into the handshake.)

P = Position

Be careful to ensure that the person with whom you are dealing does not feel trapped or hemmed in. Position yourself so that he or she has exit routes. They need to be able to see a way past you – particularly to doors etc. – when in a building or confined area. If you block the possibility of 'flight' they may see little choice but to fight.

BE AWARE

Be aware of the spatial relationship between you and the person with whom you are dealing. If you are too close then, in an innate way, a potential aggressor can feel like a cornered animal left with no choice but to lash out.

A = Attitude

Remember, your attitude will affect your behaviour and this can escalate a situation unless you work to break the cycle. No matter how negative you may feel towards the individual, show positive signals that emphasise your willingness to help and find a solution to the problem.

BE AWARE

Don't allow your own emotions to dictate the situation. Remember that you are a professional just doing a job. It's not personal, so don't make it so. If you have personal hot-spots regarding the way people talk to you, then you will find yourself responding to those insults and therefore being controlled by your emotions. It is reasonable to assume that you will not be able to control a potentially hostile situation if you cannot first control how you react.

L = Look and listen actively

Eye contact is a vital element in signalling non-aggression. In normal conversation, the listener will maintain eye contact with the speaker; the speaker will drop eye contact from time to time. In aggressive situations it is important to try to achieve as near normal eye contact as possible. Never stare fixedly at the other person, as this can seem very aggressive.

'Active listening' means demonstrating with gestures such as head-nodding, and repeating back phrases that you are hearing, to indicate that you understand what the other person is saying.

BE AWARE

I agree that you should maintain eye contact in order to show an interest in what the individual is saying; this is essential if any kind of rapport is to be achieved. However, I prefer to maintain a kind of soft focus rather than any kind of hard stare, as the latter can be seen as confrontational on your part. Also it is important to understand the need to scan actively for an additional threat, particularly if the individual you are dealing with is extremely aggressive.

In such a situation you may begin to feel the effects of adrenal stress, including tunnel vision (see Section 10.3, on fear and adrenal stress). This will cause your peripheral vision to start to close down, making you vulnerable to a threat from the side. So, yes, maintain eye contact but at the same time remain aware of what and who is around you – this includes where your exits are, should you need to remove this person, and also where obstacles and people are in relation to the route you would follow in order to take such action.

M = Make space

In normal circumstances we rarely stand 'square on' to someone when we speak to them. We tend to stand slightly to one side. In aggressive situations, standing to one side will take away the square-on effect. It also opens up visual 'exit routes' for both you and the other person.

BE AWARE

Controlling the amount of space between you is extremely important when dealing with a hostile individual. See Section 6.4 for more information on this.

S = Stance

This is covered in detail in the section dealing with proxemics and natural non-aggressive postures (Section 6.4). (The *Oxford English Dictionary* defines proxemics as the 'branch of study concerned with the amount of space that people set between themselves and others'.)

6.2 Protecting your personal space

If while dealing with an aggressive person you start to notice any of the body language cues described in Chapter 5, then you will not have much time before you may have to react to a physical assault. Whenever you deal with anyone, regardless of their intention, you should always take up a natural, non-aggressive position. Such a position will allow you to control the space between you and whomever you happen to be talking to. This will also place your hands in a position that will allow you to use defensive tactics should the need arise. (As people talk, it is usual to make small, habitual hand movements in any case, so it is natural to stand at a slight distance away from whomever you are talking to, in order to facilitate this movement.)

The final precursor to violence is the attempt to close distance. In the event of this happening during a show of aggression you should immediately attempt to re-create the space between you. Do this by placing your lead hand out as a barrier as you take a step back. If necessary, you may have to shove the aggressor back in order to regain space, but try to avoid touching them unless it is absolutely necessary. By doing this, you are taking your control of the space between you to a conscious level, so it is important that you back this up with a verbal command to help reinforce your boundary.

Use an assertive command such as 'Get back!' or 'Stay where you are!' This will alert the individual to the fact that you are prepared to defend yourself, as well as draw the attention of other members of staff to the potential situation and inform members of the public who are not involved to stay clear.

This kind of combined verbal and physical 'fence' (see Section 6.4) may act as an effective non-physical option, which of course is always the kind of option you as a door supervisor should seek to take, whenever and wherever possible.

Posturing

The act of posturing (see page 75 of Section 7.4), using simulated aggression – as controversial as some may find it – is still a non-physical option and has had enough successful application in the field to warrant its use as such. However, it is a last-ditch attempt at avoiding physical violence and is not the same as the sort of verbal assertion I have described above.

6.3 Third-party observation

This applies to what you may be heard saying by a witness as well as to any action they may see you taking. They may, for example, witness you managing aggression. If your body language and physical posture look non-aggressive and you are heard making statements such as 'Look sir, why don't you just calm down?' or 'Come on sir, let's see if we can find a sensible solution that is acceptable to all concerned', this will make it a lot less likely that a third-party observer will see you as the aggressor. Another, similar, example is when the door supervisor physically has to remove a non-compliant person from the premises.

Too often, unfortunately, you may be looked upon as heavy-handed, especially when all the public see is your physical response and they are oblivious to all the facts, including your vain attempts to conclude the situation without having to take such action. At such times it doesn't hurt to be heard saying aloud something like 'Look, just keep moving and you won't get hurt.'

Trust me when I tell you that this kind of thing can become truly relevant in the event of police involvement post-event, particularly if there is a chance that you might have to justify your actions later in a court of law.

It is my feeling that the job of the door supervisor can be something of a double-edged sword. On the one hand, you may have to contend with the element of violence that will, without doubt, involve the risk of injury or worse to you as an individual. In such a situation you may have to take whatever action is necessary to protect first yourself, then your colleagues and members of the public (using no more force than is necessary). On the other hand, after that, you may have to justify your actions to a courtroom of individuals, who will assess your actions on what *they* deem reasonable in the circumstances presented, taking into account various statements, including those of third-party observers (but minus, of course, the threat to your safety and the adrenal stress that will have accompanied the situation you found yourself in at the time). This can make the whole affair something of a grey area, to say the least, so please try to bear these elements in mind as you operate, and strive to present yourself as a confident, polite and respectable professional.

Now let's take a look at various natural-looking postures we can use to protect our own personal space.

6.4 Proxemics and situational control

Our personal space expands and contracts according to the situation we are in. This space could range from less than a foot in a crowd situation, via four or five feet while walking along the pavement, right up to 20 or more feet when walking along an empty street at night. It is very important that we protect our personal space when dealing with a potentially aggressive individual. We do this by using a natural non-aggressive-looking posture commonly called the 'fence'. This will allow you enough time to defuse a hostile situation verbally and will also, in a worst-case scenario, act as a platform from which to launch your pre-emptive physical response.

This simple concept was introduced to the martial arts scene during the early 1990s by veteran doorman/martial artist and writer Geoff Thompson, who worked the doors in Coventry during the 1980s at a time when it was considered one of the most violent cities in England. Although Geoff won't take credit for the invention of this idea, he is certainly responsible for its development and title. The following descriptions and illustrations run through some suggested natural stances that also offer a good foundation for quickly responding to physical action. Which one you use will depend on the situation and where the aggressor is standing just before things get physical.

Outside touching distance

This is a good way to stand when the distance between you is at arm's length plus a step before engagement (see Figure 6.1). This is known as your circle of defence. Note that the arms are across the body but not folded. The feet are in a natural and well-balanced position. In this position the door supervisor is aware of the aggressor and ready for action.

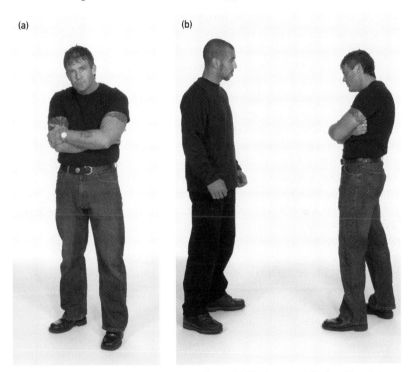

(a)   (b)

Figure 6.1 The fence: outside touching distance

A small 45-degree stance is preserved by placing one foot in front of the other and 'blading' the body away from the potential aggressor, in order to present less of a target. In all of these natural stances the aim is to look non-aggressive while placing your hands in a position so that they are higher than the aggressor's. This is also a good posture to adopt as a third-party observer – watching the back of a colleague for example.

Touching distance

This is conversation range (see Figure 6.2). Here you've got no more than a two-foot gap between you and whomever you are dealing with. This is how the majority of your dealings with the general public, including those who display aggressive behaviour, will take place. The worst position that you could be in at this range or closer is to have your hands down by your sides or in your pockets. It is absolutely essential that your hands are kept up, protecting the space between you both. If they're not, the aggressor will be in your face before you can do anything.

The position you should take up is as follows. The feet are placed in a small 45-degree position that allows you to blade your body away from your potential aggressor, so that you are again presenting him with less of a target. Both hands are open and can be held in a variety of non-aggressive-looking positions; the important thing is that they occupy the space between you both. It's also important to note that the fence is not held static; instead the hands move in and out while controlling the distance between you both, as if you are talking with your hands. This will allow you to relieve the stress of the situation while giving you some degree of control. You have the option from here to use verbal dialogue to talk the person down or, if necessary, as a distraction and verbal trigger before your own pre-emptive action.

The fence is difficult to depict through photographs without making it appear static. In all cases when operating from the fence, it is important that you keep your hands moving in and out in order to occupy the space between you both. You should do this as you are talking, with your hands moving around and changing places intermittently (see Figure 6.3).

When using the fence the lead hand serves three functions.

Figure 6.2 The fence: touching distance

(a)　　　　　(b)

Figure 6.3 Using the fence leaves the lead hand ready to serve several functions

1. **It controls space:** Without the fence the space between you and a potential threat will be closed in an instant, and followed by a possible assault.

2. **It acts as a feeler hand:** This tells you when a possible assault is imminent. If the aggressor moves forward aggressively or attempts to slap your hands out of the way he is revealing his intention to attack. This is why it is so important to control this space. Any attempt at closing the gap should be checked with your lead hand by shoving the individual away as you take a step back to maintain the space between you both. This should be backed up with a firm verbal boundary, such as 'Stay where you are!' followed by a pointing finger or a stop-sign gesture. This show of force on your part tells the individual that his next show of aggression will be met with resistance. It's important for him to understand that his next attempt at closing the gap will be met with physical action on your part. The action that you take from the fence depends on the level of threat you are facing. If trying to talk him down fails, it is probable that physical restraint may be required.

3. **It acts as a range finder:** This means that if your lead hand can touch him then your rear hand can strike. If the aggressor is a real threat then the only safe option is to strike pre-emptively.

The de-escalation stance

In my experience this is the best position to adopt if the person you are dealing with is extremely aggressive right from the off. As I have already mentioned, things can go from talking to violence in a heartbeat, in which case this position is the ideal one to operate from. The exact position that I have found useful is to raise both hands at about chin level, with my palms facing the potential assailant (see Figure 6.4); my body language is telling

(a)

(b)

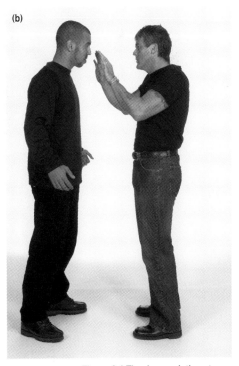

Figure 6.4 The de-escalation stance

him 'Calm down and let's talk'. My hands may be in line, or I may have one slightly in front of the other. This is kind of subservient-looking, good for de-escalation, as well for striking should this be required.

It's a stance that allows a fair degree of situational control and, by placing my hands higher than his I am in an ideal position to employ a physical response should my verbal dissuasion fail.

Extreme close quarters (ECQ)

As a door supervisor you may find yourself in a situation where you are closer to the aggressor than is ideal. Often it will be the noise level that dictates this distance – dealing with an individual on the dancefloor, for example, or in a crowded environment such as at a concert or sporting event. In such a situation you will have to modify your fence into a shortened version. There are a couple of alternatives that I have found effective at this range. Keep the same balanced foot position, place one hand on your chin and the other under your elbow, folded loosely across your body, as if deep in thought (see Figure 6.5). From this position you'll notice that you appear non-aggressive but are ready to strike instantly. Your hands can be used defensively as well as offensively.

Again this is also a good position from which to observe as a third party and will also work well if the potential aggressor is standing at your flank.

(a)

(b)

Figure 6.5 Modified fence for ECQ situations (option 1)

Another approach is to hold your hands loosely together (not interlocking your fingers) just in front of your lower chest area (see Figure 6.6).

Whichever method you use, it's important to keep a balanced foot position, also blade your body to 45 degrees and drop your head slightly forward, with your chin close to your chest. This way, if he tries to head-butt you, his face will meet the top of your head. Try to create space as soon as you can or, if necessary, act pre-emptively from here.

Figure 6.6 Modified fence for ECQ situations (option 2)

Again this is not static (see Figure 6.7); rather, my hands are making small movements as I move each of them in and out intermittently, controlling the gap between us.

Tactile fence

Sometimes, when dealing with people, you will find that the distance between you both is dictated by your environment. If you have to talk to someone on a loud and busy dancefloor, for example, chances are that you won't be able to hear each other. This will create the need to get so close that you are practically talking in the potential aggressor's ear. There is a danger here, particularly if you are dealing with hostility right from the start.

Figure 6.7 Modified fence for ECQ situations (option 3)

The best way to operate in this situation is to get close to the individual and slightly to his flank (see Figure 6.8). Use your hands in a very tactile way, placing the flat of your lead hand very lightly onto the outside of his upper right arm. Make sure that the touch is really light, not tight and controlling.

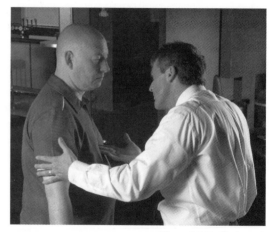

Figure 6.8 Tactile fence 1

Now use your right hand (palm turned up as if in exclamation) to control the gap between you both (see Figure 6.9a). Strive to talk to the individual in a calm but firm tone. Keep your head down slightly to avoid the potential for an attempted head-butt or bite from this close proximity.

Figure 6.9b depicts the person holding a bottle (potential weapon) being monitored at the hand.

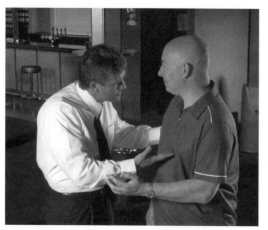

(a)

(b)

Figure 6.9 Tactile fence 2

BE AWARE

This way of using your hands, in a tactile way, will allow you to read the potential aggressor's intention through touch and sensitivity, and to feel any tension or sudden aggressive movement from his arms or other parts of his body. This provides you with an early-warning signal should the subject start to get physical.

CHAPTER SEVEN

NON-PHYSICAL OPTIONS

7.1 Introduction

The information in this chapter aims to provide you with an array of non-physical options that will, to all intents and purposes, allow you to work to the best of your ability in terms of defusing the majority of potentially hostile situations you are likely to face.

The material in this chapter is based on the requirements of the current SIA training course (including the SAFER and POP models, see page 68) as well as methods that have proved themselves effective with a large number of door- and event-security people who have worked in this field for a number of years.

As with the physical options that we will look at in the next chapter, some of the methods described here may provoke a degree of controversy. Just bear in mind that, although these are born out of real experience and based on successful outcomes, they are nonetheless to be viewed as guidelines only.

7.2 Effective communication skills

- Show an understanding of basic communication skills
- Show an understanding of verbal and non-verbal communication
- Show an understanding of some blocks to communication
- State how to deal with customers with mental illness

(SIA definition)

As a door supervisor, it is impossible to avoid conflict completely while you are doing your job. For this reason, it is important to understand how to deal with conflict and aggression when they occur. Good communication skills are absolutely vital to defusing conflict, so you need to understand how we communicate. You also need to recognise the 'blocks' that make it difficult for people to understand each other and that get in the way of effective communication. We communicate in other ways apart from speaking, and non-verbal communication is very important in emotional and threatening situations.

The basics of communication

The basic elements of communication are as follows: when someone has something in his/her head to pass to you, he/she creates a coded message – usually made up of words (the actual words spoken), tone (the way the words are spoken) and non-verbal behaviour, or body language (see below). You then have to decode the message and reply with one of your own.

Non-verbal behaviour/body language

Many studies have been done about communication and it is generally accepted that in a face-to-face situation the meaning of a message is gained by the receiver as follows:

- words – 7%
- tone – 38%
- communication/body language – 55%.

It is clear, then, that your words will make little impact unless your tone and body language match what you are saying. Effective communication influences behaviour, and good communication skills will allow you to take control of situations and people.

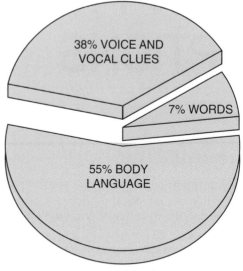

Figure 7.1 How the receiver deduces the meaning of a message

Matching your body language and tone to your words
Remember:

- your body language and tone of voice will make a big impact
- it's not so much what you say – it's how you say it
- if you try to understand the other person's point of view this will ease communication.

What is my body language saying?
Some body language can make people feel threatened. Any gestures that might be interpreted as aggressive should be avoided while you are trying to de-escalate a situation. Such gestures might include the following.

- Finger-pointing or finger-wagging gestures usually go with 'being told off' and can therefore be humiliating.
- Crossing your arms: standing with your arms crossed can make you look defensive. You should keep your posture natural and non-aggressive-looking, while still allowing you to control the space around you (proxemics).
- Sudden or quick movements of your arms: if the person you are talking to is jumpy or nervous, they might misinterpret any sudden movements as an attack.
- Rolling your eyes skyward: this gesture, combined with raising your eyebrows and rolling your head back is a sign of irritation and impatience.
- Looking down on people: lowering your eyes rather than your head to look at someone can make people feel you are 'looking down on them' or suggesting they are stupid.

- Frowning or scowling: if you look unfriendly, fed up or miserable, this will affect the people you are dealing with.

Positive communication

Positive communication prevents conflict. You can go a long way towards preventing conflict by:

- looking and sounding professional
- acting consistently and fairly
- working effectively with your colleagues as a team.

Triggers and inhibitors

Triggers are small things that, when combined with other problems, spark off aggression. They are 'the last straw that breaks the camel's back'. So if a person is already feeling frustrated by long waits, poor service or personal circumstance, there are many triggers that are likely to spark off a reaction. You can never know what someone has been through just before their encounter with you. So you should not be surprised when an apparently small thing makes a customer very angry.

Common triggers

People tend to be 'triggered' into an angry reaction if they feel:

- embarrassed
- humiliated
- insulted
- afraid
- rejected.

Customers may feel like this when they think someone else is talking down to them, ignoring them or not taking them seriously. If you make the mistake of not treating customers with respect at all times, they may use your unprofessional attitude as an excuse for their own bad behaviour. Their behaviour may be much worse than yours, but they can still say that you started it.

Inhibitors

Inhibitors are things that prevent people from completely losing their temper – they inhibit aggression. We know that not everybody gets violent when they become angry; this is because we all have inhibitors based on:

- self-control
- personal values
- fear that the other person will fight back
- social or legal consequences
- experience
- training.

How the wrong choice can escalate the problem

Your choice of action is important. Even when you have passed the 'fight or flight' stage you still have a choice between escalating or de-escalating the situation. When you are feeling angry, emotional or tense, you may easily do or say something that will make matters worse. A smart comment, or a pointing or poking finger, could trigger an escalation. You need to choose consciously to deal with the incident so that no one feels humiliated or gets more wound up or frustrated. As noted before, behaviour breeds behaviour.

Don't let negative feelings show

It is very difficult to change your attitude towards someone. It is, however, possible to change the way you behave towards them. You can learn to behave so that your negative feelings do not show, so that your behaviour doesn't reflect your negative feelings. This breaks the cycle and stops things getting worse.

7.3 Workable models for risk assessment

One of the most important ways of avoiding conflict is to be able to recognise the potential threat in a situation. You then need to assess the situation so that you can respond appropriately, control how it develops and reduce the risk of being involved in conflict. In this section, we will look at some practical ways of doing this.

The SAFER approach (an SIA model)

Using the SAFER model will help you to evaluate a potentially threatening situation and choose the best response.

- **S** = **Step back** – don't rush into a situation, stop and think.
- **A** = **Assess threat** – identify potential dangers (see the POP approach, below).
- **F** = **Find help** – think about what help you may need, or who you need to communicate with.
- **E** = **Evaluate your options** – decide what options are available to you and choose the one most likely to work.
- **R** = **Respond** – when you have done all of the above, take your chosen course of action, then continue to assess the threat and change your approach if necessary.

Rational thought and POP assessment (an SIA model)

The emergency services use a simple but effective system for assessing the threat presented by a person, object or place. This is known as the POP approach. Using the POP model you can assess the potential threat of a situation by using rational thought processes. Once you have assessed a threat, any decisions you make can also be thought through rationally. By applying rational thought you will avoid acting on impulse.

POP involves breaking threats down into three categories or types, as outlined below.

Person (P)

Assess the situation with regard to the person, or people, involved.

- Are they suffering from the effects of drink/drugs/mental disorder?
- Are they bigger/fitter/younger/stronger than you?
- What is their emotional state?
- Who are the other people present and who are they likely to support?
- If you have met these people before, what do you know about them?
- Do they have a history of anger/aggression?
- Are they known criminals?
- Have they had a bad experience of your organisation?

Object (O)

Next, assess the situation with regard to any objects you know are present or likely to be present, for example:

- front door/points of access
- apparently innocuous articles, such as glasses, syringes, combs, bottles, cans, that could be used as offensive weapons
- knives and other edged weapons
- moving vehicles.

Place (P)

Finally, assess the situation from the point of view of the location and environment you are in. Some places are more threatening than others: for example, remote areas – away from the observation of others – or refuges such as toilets, stairwells and car parks. Here are some more examples:

- routes to and from work
- dark areas or places where there are flashing lights
- areas that are full of people but where you find you are the only door supervisor.

A location can present different threats depending on time of day or night.

Using POP you will also be able to explain to another person how threatening the situation was and why you responded in the way you did. This could be very important if you have to give evidence in court.

The dangers of complacency

We tend to respond quickly to high-risk situations where the threat is obvious – for example, when someone is shouting and threatening us with a broken bottle. We can be more vulnerable when we underestimate, or do not realise, the threat presented by the situation.

Often you will know very little about the person(s) you are dealing with, which means you are dealing with an unknown risk; so treat them with respect and an element of caution.

BE AWARE

Regardless of the situation, if you have been offered a show of aggression by anyone, always assume that they have the potential to be carrying a weapon and that there might be more than one aggressor.

The importance of communication

In order to reassure a customer that you are really listening to what they are saying, it is important to:

- focus your attention on them
- use non-verbal cues (e.g. nodding the head)
- show that you have understood; say things like 'OK, let me see if I've understood this correctly …', and then paraphrase what they have said
- maintain appropriate eye contact; this reinforces the non-verbal message that we are paying attention to what is being said
- let them finish speaking before you act; never interrupt or cut across a person's speech
- ask open questions (i.e. questions that don't lend themselves to simple yes/no answers – when, where, how etc.)
- ask them to explain anything that is unclear or confusing
- be patient.

If several people are talking at once, you may need to control the situation first in order to ensure that you can listen to each in turn.

Outside your work environment you probably have a choice about whether or not to confront behaviour that is unacceptable to you. As a door supervisor you have a duty to act and a responsibility to your employers to manage problems as they arise. You will have to deal with people whose behaviour is 'unacceptable'. They may be shouting and swearing, making it very difficult for you to do your job, and upsetting other customers.

Confronting them could easily lead to the escalation of an already difficult and risky situation. If you feel you have to confront, then make sure you are assertive rather than aggressive. Many people make the mistake of thinking assertive behaviour is similar to aggressive behaviour. An example of a good assertive statement is:

I understand why you are angry, but if you continue to shout and swear, you leave me no option but to ask you to leave, which I don't want to have to do.

This shows empathy with the individual and respects the other person's position, but clearly states what is unacceptable and what will happen if it doesn't stop. It is important to make sure your body language gives a similar message: you might make a good assertive statement but turn it aggressive by 'squaring on' or pointing.

The REACT model (a police model)

You can use the acronym REACT to give you guidance on the escalating level of control that may be employed during a potentially confrontational situation:

- **R**equest
- **E**xplain
- **A**ppeal
- **C**onfirm
- **T**ake action

The first stage is to **request** – that is, ask the customer to comply (e.g. leave the premises). As a door supervisor you will find that the majority of people will do as they are asked, particularly if your conduct is polite and your request reasonable. It is inevitable, however, that some people will not comply, and will instead stand there and argue until they are blue in the face, in an attempt to get their own way.

It is important at this point that you make sure that the customer understands what you are asking of them. So you should now **explain**, giving a reason according to whatever law or house policy has been breached or the behaviour that has caused you to request the customer to leave the premises. Should this still be met with non-compliance then you should repeat the request and **appeal** to the customer to do what you have asked, explaining what action will be taken unless your request is met.

For the sake of this example, let's say the customer refuses to leave; he will therefore have to be physically evicted from the premises and the police may have to be called. If the individual still refuses to comply then you will need to prepare for the use of reasonable force. Just before doing so it is recommended that you **confirm** that this person completely understands, bringing in such phrases as 'Is there anything I can do or say that will make you change your mind?' This will offer them one final escape route via which they may comply without losing face (see also the sections on 'loop-holing' and 'the honourable escape route', below). It will also completely justify the use of reasonable force should they not take that route.

The final stage, if all your powers of persuasion have failed, is to **take action**. In this example it is recommended that you summon assistance and physically evict the individual from the premises. The REACT model has given them four opportunities to comply before physical action is taken. If this step-by-step approach is followed before you use any level of force during the course of your duty, then you should be able to answer satisfactorily any questions relating to the justification of your actions.

The violent minority

The majority of people who frequent our pubs and nightclubs do so in pursuit of a good night out, but you need to be aware that there also exists a violent minority. In some situations, an aggressor may escalate a situation from the **request** stage of the REACT model to a point where physical **action** is imminently required, in a heartbeat.

The fact of the matter is that, as beneficial as all these models are (and, indeed, each one has its place and has proved effective in controlling such situations in the past), the violent minority will always mistake politeness for weakness. Such individuals may well see the four opportunities for compliance that you have offered them as a chink in your armour which they will then seek to exploit.

It is your duty as a door supervisor to strive to employ such non-physical options as are suggested here, but do bear in mind that some situations can escalate into violence straight away, leaving you no time whatsoever for talking. So build this in to your game plan. It would be nice to think that, if you are reasonable, those you are dealing with will respond in the same way; in a lot of cases this is so, but it is not the case with all of the people all of the time.

As I've said a couple of times before, wherever you find people and alcohol you have a recipe for aggression and violence. This has been a fact of life from the days of the old-school bouncer – and that's without adding the effects of drugs and mental health problems to the mix.

So, whatever happens, stay switched on and be polite and professional. Strive to educate yourself and develop the skills and confidence that will carry you through the more difficult situations and you will find your work one of the most character-building jobs you could do.

7.4 De-escalation skills

Talking a situation down

Most situations where you are faced with hostility can be managed effectively by calmly 'talking the situation down'. In a lot of cases, all that is necessary is to get the aggressor's attention by finding their motivation and then trying to build a rapport with them so that you can strive to defuse the situation – for example, 'Look sir, let's just see if we can find a suitable solution to this problem that will be acceptable to yourself and all concerned.' With reasonable people, this kind of tactic will work just fine.

Verbal dissuasion

Defusing a potentially dangerous situation by means of talking is known as verbal dissuasion, or de-escalation. The goal of de-escalation is to try and resolve a potentially hostile situation without having to resort to any physical action. De-escalation skills are useful when dealing with people who are highly agitated, frustrated, angry, fearful or intoxicated.

The person in question might be someone that you know, who is normally a peaceful individual but is simply responding to unusual or extreme circumstances with negative aggression. Or you may have to work with members of the general public on a daily basis, in which case verbal dissuasion can come in very handy when dealing with an agitated person.

Remember, however, that de-escalation skills are a non-physical option. If you find yourself in a situation where an imminent attack on your person is apparent and obvious – such as a mugging attempt, attempted abduction or sexual assault – then obviously a physical response, preferably pre-emptive, would be the best option. The following principles should be observed and put into practice if verbal dissuasion is to be used effectively.

- **Project a confident and attentive demeanour:** Maintain eye contact and try to avoid averting your gaze as this could be taken as a lack of interest or regard, or rejection. The idea is to try and find the source of the individual's agitation and quickly establish a rapport with them. So be sure to stay attentive, but at the same time try to avoid staring, which can appear threatening.
- **Mirror calm:** Control your own level of arousal. Emotions can interfere with your own mental and physical function as well as those of the person that you're dealing with. A low to moderate level of arousal will keep you alert and ready to take action should the need arise. Correct breathing will help you to control anxiety under stress. A lot of people tend to hold their breath or breathe very shallowly during times of stress, which serves only to increase their anxiety. Instead try to breathe deeply, right down into your diaphragm and not just in your chest (see the information on breathing control in Section 10.4). A good cadence is to breathe in for three seconds, hold for two, and then breathe out for another three seconds. This will help to lower your heart rate and keep you calm. Don't make this obvious, though – try to keep it as natural-looking as possible.
- **Positive self-talk:** It is human nature to allow negative thinking and self-doubt to creep in; we do this by sending undermining messages to ourselves, such as 'I'm in trouble now' or 'I can't handle this situation.' All such thoughts must be ignored and erased from your thinking. One way to do this is to counter them with positive self-talk. Tell yourself 'I can handle it; for better or for worse I will handle anything.'

BE AWARE

If you practise deep, slow breathing and positive self-talk regularly, in response to any form of stress or anxiety in your daily life, you will be more likely to respond in this way when dealing with a potentially hostile individual. In other words, this calming behaviour will become your conditioned response to danger, which will in turn allow you to project confidence. It may also have a calming effect on your potential aggressor.

Protect your personal space: Make sure that you use a non-aggressive-looking fence posture, or a similar natural stance, which will also serve as a launch pad for your pre-emptive strike should a physical option become necessary.

Loop-holing

This is the sort of technique you use when you talk to the awkward individual's mate or girlfriend, and try to get them to talk the situation down, or talk their friend into leaving the premises, should your attempt at verbal dissuasion fail. You could say something like:

Look, why don't you take your friend home now? My manager is literally seconds away from phoning our mobile security unit and they won't be as understanding as I am. The police will be right behind them and anyone who is left causing a problem will be spending the night in the cells.

The honourable escape route

Another example of loop-holing is giving your aggressor an honourable escape route. A lot of times, this kind of person does not really want to get physical, he is just sounding off for the benefit of his mates or a female companion, driven by 'ego gratification'. He doesn't really want to fight, but ego continues to fuel his aggression.

An obvious consideration here is that Mr Awkward Customer will be a lot more sensitive about losing face if he is within earshot of his companions. In such a case you will have more chance of defusing the situation if you can separate the individual from the rest of his group. Offer a gesture to him to follow you, and suggest a word in private. This could be said firmly and with authority in front of his mates so he feels compelled to follow you or risk losing face right there. Or you could put your arm around him in a friendly kind of gesture and pull him to one side, out of earshot of his friends. Once there, suggest to him that it is nothing personal, but you are just doing your job and he has got to leave, but if he wants to make it physical, then you will humiliate him by kicking seven shades of shit out of him in front of everyone.

If he's all talk, it's at this point that you will see doubt and fear in his face, in which case offer him the honourable escape route. Suggest that he tell his friends that, as a personal favour to the door supervisor, he will leave quietly. That way he hasn't lost face and does not have to fight. If, however, your suggestions are met with aggression, then, as in all cases, be prepared to back them up with the physical. This method was used a lot by Geoff Thompson during his ten years of door work in some of the worst pubs and clubs in Coventry, which, as I mentioned in an earlier chapter, was without doubt one of the most violent cities in Britain at that time.

I have also found loop-holing effective. One shift I worked was on what they call a 'dance boat party' that sailed around the Solent until two in the morning. A certain individual decided to kick off for the benefit of his mates, so I deceptively led him out on to the deck, out the way of his friends. At this point I grabbed his collar and shoved him off-balance against the barrier giving him a bird's eye view of the sea. I told him that if he played up again he would be swimming home, but that if he went back inside and told his mates that, as a personal favour to me, he was going to behave for the rest of the night, I would be very grateful to him. Of course, no one but he and I would need to know how he shrieked like a little girl while taking a closer look at the sea. Needless to say, I didn't hear a peep out of him for the rest of the night.

The tactful approach

Another method involves the use of tact. For example, if you're on the door and a guy looking like a drunken slob walks up seeking entry to your venue, you don't insult him by telling him that's why he's not coming in – that would be rude and unnecessary. Instead, use a little tact. Tell him that it's a members-only night. He might guess that you're lying, but at least it gives him the chance to leave without losing face. If he challenges your refusal, stick to the members-only excuse, but add that you think he's had too much to drink.

Another way to loop-hole is to tell the awkward individual that, due to the fact that you happen to be an extremely fair person, you would rather advise them of the possible consequences if they carry on being a nuisance and/or aggressive, rather than have to call the police and have them locked in a cell for the night with the possibility of a court hearing the next day. In addition, you should inform them that their face has already been caught on CCTV, which is linked to the local police and security network, regardless of whether it is or not. If such a ploy works on just one individual then it has proved its worth as a non-physical option.

Posturing

The following option may cause some degree of controversy. But in the past, posturing has proved so effective for resolving conflict without violence – not just for me but for literally scores of door staff that I know and have worked with – that it simply cannot be ignored for its value as a non-physical option.

Posturing is the art of 'psyching out' your opponent by the use of words, tone and body language. The effect that this can cause will often send your potential aggressor the signal that if he continues to instigate aggression and violence in your presence, it will be to his own detriment. There are two basic approaches that you can use in order to achieve this aim: the veteran approach and the psych-out approach. We will now take a look at each of these in turn.

The veteran approach

Here your demeanour is so calm and confident that the individual will know that you are more than capable of dealing with troublesome individuals such as him if he continues to push it. No matter how aggressive and agitated your potential threat becomes, you will act with calm while wearing an emotionless expression that says you have been here many times before, and with a lot bigger and better than him.

Such a role, properly played out, will often cause your potential opponent to doubt his own ability. If he is trying to intimidate you through his aggressive behaviour and lack of regard for your position, and you make it clear to him that this just isn't working, then it is quite likely that he will have second thoughts. The usual response to someone suddenly realising they have bitten off more than they can chew is for them suddenly to start back-pedalling.

Most times this will be accompanied by some kind of self-redeeming comment, such as 'Yeah, well, I'll see you again' or 'You'd better watch your back, mate.' What this person is really telling you is that he has just lost his bottle and is backing off, but is trying to save a little face as he does so. That's fine – take no notice of what he says and don't say anything to make the situation personal. Stay ever-vigilant and let him go. A situation avoided is a situation won.

The use of posturing usually comes into play if verbal dissuasion is failing or, for whatever reason, you don't quite feel that a physical response is needed yet. It can also be useful if you sense that your opponent is not as confident as he makes out and you feel that he can indeed be psyched out. Mouthing off while standing outside touching range, or as the individual walks away, is a clear indication of this. If the individual moves forwards while displaying aggression, or acts in a deceptively friendly manner in order to get close, then this clearly indicates the opposite. In such cases, a physical assault is highly probable so be prepared to take physical action first if need be.

It is important that you understand these kinds of attack rituals and the deceptive ploys that people will often use, and act on them accordingly (see the discussion of attack rituals in Section 5.5, page 50). Posturing is usually a last-ditch attempt before a physical response is required. If the aggressor has already encroached on your personal space by slapping your hands aside or moving forwards aggressively, then he has already revealed his intentions.

Remember, the final precursor to violence is the attempt to close the distance between you both. At this point you really must act. Posturing can prevent a conflict from entering the physical arena. The thing to bear in mind is that, once you posture, you have shown your hand. Any chance of acting pre-emptively in the physical sense via deception has now passed. The truth is that most would-be aggressors are looking for a victim, not someone that is prepared to give them the fight of their lives.

The only way you will ever know for sure if your aggressor is all noise or a serious threat is to take him right to the door of potential violence. In my experience the majority of people will back away, leaving the serious minority who will take you up on it. This really isn't a case of 'If you can't fight, wear a big hat.' You must always be prepared physically to back up your position with everything you have should your bluff be called. The way to look at it is, if you posture and make it work, you will have ended the conflict without a fight; if not, and your aggressor takes you up on it, well then, you would have been fighting anyway.

Acting in a cool and confident manner in the face of an aggressive individual (while protecting your personal space and being ever-prepared to strike first should the need arise) sends out a signal that you are a capable individual who has been along this path many times before, and this in turn will plant the seed of doubt in your aggressor's mind, undermining his ability to intimidate you.

The psych-out approach

This requires an explosive display of aggression on your part. Some people are better at this kind of thing than others – it's just a matter of combining the three elements of **voice**, **touch** and **stare** to create the right chemistry. I have seen people create total and utter capitulation in their recipient just by looking at them across a crowded room. If you have a face that looks like a pit bull terrier licking piss off a nettle then you can create this kind of effect with just a look. If not, then it is a personal decision as to whether or not you decide to employ this kind of tactic. Again, if you feel there is a chink in your aggressor's armour and you have truly exhausted the nicely-nicely approach to no avail, then aggressive posturing is an effective and proven non-physical option.

Figure 7.2 shows the sort of sequence a typical psych-out approach will run through. From your non-aggressive posture, explode into your aggressor with a sharp shove to the centre of his chest using the flat palms of both hands. You are not striking him, this is just a shove performed very explosively that will create instant space between you and him. This action will trigger his flight response and cause him to dump adrenalin. You should combine this shove with a very loud and aggressive verbal boundary such as 'Get back now or you're down!'

Understand that, in the real world, there may be a need to back up your statement with expletives. Swearing is street-speak and the language of contemporary combat – nobody creates dominance with words such as 'cad' or 'blighter'. The 'F word' and the 'C word'

Figure 7.2 The psych-out approach: sequence of actions

bear malice and add impact to a statement. I'm not *telling* you to use such language, I am merely saying that's the way it is. You have to ask yourself: do you want to be taken seriously or not?

Any verbal boundary should be backed up with a firm physical fence, keeping both hands in the formation of a stop sign – or, to make it sharper, a pointing-finger gesture – while maintaining a hard, crazy stare that says 'Don't mess' in any language. In this way, the three elements of touch, voice and stare are combined. The dialogue may need to be continued in the form of offering the recipient consequences, such as 'You step up again and you're *down*!'

To sum up ...

As I said before, this is a controversial subject and some of my suggestions would probably make the majority of the members of our licensing body cringe in disapproval but, at the end of the day, I am offering you non-physical options that have been employed on many, many occasions with great success.

So, decide for yourself – the information provided here is merely an offering. The main thing to bear in mind is that posturing really can be the art of fighting without fighting. However, just in case your bluff is called, always be prepared to back it up with the physical action required to parallel the threat you are facing.

CHAPTER EIGHT

PHYSICAL OPTIONS

8.1 Introduction

The last option available to you, should your attempts at talking down, loop-holing or psyching-out the individual fail, is the physical. If the person you're dealing with has left you no other option, then don't think twice: remember that your safety is your priority, no matter what your employer may say. I've come across some who have said that you must wait to be attacked, or even hit, before you have the right to launch any attempt at restraint – they've no idea what real-life violence is like! That sort of thinking *will* get you hurt. If you are dealing with a large aggressor, drunk and pissed off, the safest option is unconsciousness (his, obviously) via a pre-emptive strike. As far as the law is concerned, you have a right to hit first if you believe that you are at risk of being attacked and you genuinely fear for your safety.

If you honestly believe that it's all going to kick off, then action most definitely beats reaction and the best defence is a good offence. That said, if you are dealing with someone who does not appear to pose a major threat and you feel you could grab him and manhandle him out of the door restraint-style, then that's fine. Remember: use only the level of force that is necessary according to the threat you are facing – this rule applies in *all* situations.

If such 'necessary force' calls for hitting that individual first, and so hard that you totally readjust his attitude, then that's the force needed for you to be safe. From there you could follow up with restraint, as in Figure 8.1 (see also Section 8.2). In my opinion, and from my experience, the only way I have found restraints to be effective against a high-threat individual is when they are preceded by a distraction like a groin slap, body shot or knee strike to the thigh. Such actions would then make it possible to apply an effective restraint. This is the only way I would use restraint unless I was dealing with a low-threat individual.

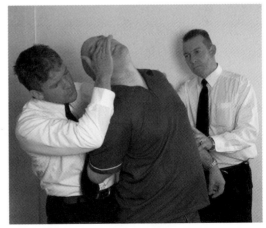

Figure 8.1 Follow up 'necessary force' with effective restraint

8.2 Workable subject control and restraint

The methods of restraint we'll look at in this section are the ones that I have found the most workable for me in 'live' situations. They originate from a variety of sources. To keep things simple, I am going to suggest only a few individual restraint techniques working from an arm-holding, 'come along' position and also from the fence. What I will also do is offer some varying level-of-force options within each of the restraints described. I will also address the matter of 'What if it goes wrong?'

The 'come along' restraint

Let's start by looking at the come-along position. This should be familiar to most door staff. Start by taking hold of the aggressor's wrist and elbow, and turn him/her so that he/she is off-centre (as illustrated in Figure 8.2). From here attempt to lead them in the direction of the exit. When walking someone out of a building, you should place them offside from you and take hold of their arm at the wrist and elbow. By holding their arm in this way you limit their attacking capability and open up their centre line, making all their major target areas accessible should you need to strike. It will also give you the benefit of tactile awareness, which allows you to use sensitivity to feel the aggressor's intention. For example, if an aggressor doesn't make a fuss about me holding their arm in this way, chances are I can just walk them out the door without a problem. However, if they decide to get aggressive then I will instantly, and literally, feel their intention and be able to respond accordingly. From there I can go to an arm lock via distraction, or if the threat is high I could strike.

(a) (b)

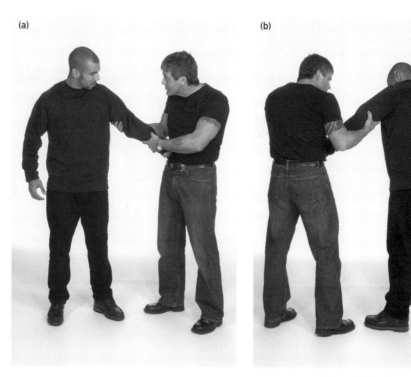

Figure 8.2 The 'come along' restraint

BE AWARE

In all cases of restraint and exit, be sure to scan actively for further threat and remain vigilant in terms of your surroundings. In all cases described here, it is assumed that you already know where your nearest exits are, and that you are aware of any obstacles (e.g. people, tables and chairs) before you make any attempt to evict the problem individual. This is where the use of a pre-planned game plan for all situations will allow you to operate to the best of your ability.

8.3 Level-of-force options

Level of force: option 1

This is a method that I would use either on a woman or a man of, say, medium build that I had already assessed and considered a low-threat individual. Start by holding the person's arm (in the example in Figure 8.3 his left arm) with your right hand on his/her elbow and your left hand on their wrist, as described in the come-along position (see above).

(a)   (b)

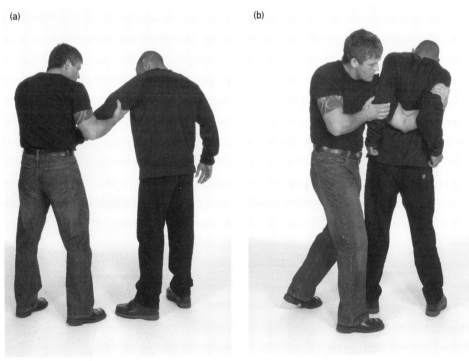

Figure 8.3 Level of force: option 1 (rear view)

From here pull the individual sharply towards you. As you do, thread your left arm through the inside of their elbow, behind their back, as you grab the inside of their right elbow with your left hand. You now have a tight hold of both arms. (The photographs in Figure 8.4 depict the same restraint from the front.)

(a)

(b)

Figure 8.4 Level of force: option 1 (front view)

This will then leave your right arm free to control their head using their hair or philtrum (under their nose). In either case, be sure to pull their head right back until it touches your shoulder and places them up on their toes (see Figure 8.5). If you use the nose to control the head then be sure to use just your first two fingers, keeping the rest clear of the mouth to avoid being bitten. From here you can walk the person sideways or backwards out of the nearest exit.

Level of force: option 2

If an individual had displayed aggression as soon as I took hold of their arm – this could be in the form of pulling away sharply or tensing up, while shouting obscenities –at this point I would find it necessary to introduce a painful distraction that would allow me to apply an effective restraint, in this case an arm lock.

Figure 8.5 Level of force: option 1 (head control)

(a)

(b)

Figure 8.6 Level of force: option 2 (creating a painful distraction)

Looking at Figure 8.6, you will see that, from the off-centre hold, my right hand maintains a grip on his left arm at the elbow as I release my left hand from his wrist. From here I explode a left elbow strike with my full body weight behind it, using the point of my elbow into his bicep muscle.

The strike to the arm will temporarily disable the limb (dead-arm effect) (see Figure 8.7),

Figure 8.7 Level of force: option 2 (taking advantage of the dead-arm effect)

allowing me to tie up the arm with a left hammerlock (Figure 8.8a). From here I finish the control by placing the fingers of my left hand (again avoiding the mouth) under his nose and pulling his head back onto my shoulder until he is up on his toes (Figure 8.8b). I am sure to keep everything tight and him close to me as I walk him, sideways or backwards, to the nearest exit. In addition, I am also using him as cover and, by walking him backwards or in a sideways direction, he cannot roll out of the control or kick back with his feet.

(a)   (b)

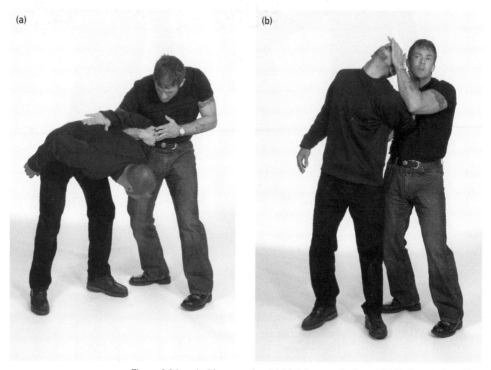

Figure 8.8 Level of force: option 2 (a) left hammerlock and (b) final control position

An alternative painful distraction

An alternative strike I have found very effective in this situation is the groin slap. This might be a light shot or a full-on strike, depending on the situation, but either will provide an effective distraction before the restraint is applied, allowing the aggressor's arm to be tied up with the hammerlock arm restraint.

Again, if you use the nose to control the head (Figure 8.9), be sure to use just your first two fingers, keeping the rest clear of the mouth to avoid being bitten. From here you can then walk the person sideways or backwards out of the nearest exit.

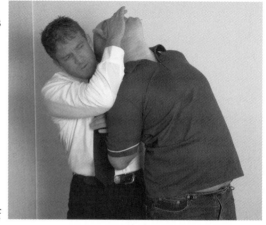

Figure 8.9 Using the nose (philtrum) to control the head

BE AWARE

Remember, where possible, always seek assistance and work with a colleague (Figure 8.10). This is important for several reasons. First, group restraint is more functional and safer for all parties concerned. Second, this offers the benefit of third-party observation and it is always helpful to have someone to act as a witness. At the very least, a fellow door supervisor should be on hand to watch your back and help you get the person clear to the exit.

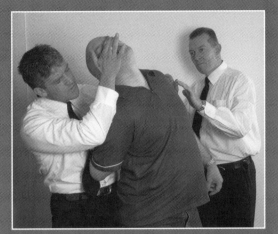

Figure 8.10 Always seek assistance and work with a colleague if possible

What if it goes wrong?

We will now look at what to do if any method of restraint starts to go wrong. In the example illustrated (Figure 8.11), if after the elbow shot to the arm or the slap to the groin you are still finding it a struggle to lock up your aggressor, on no account wrestle with him or you

Figure 8.11 Regaining control when a restraint starts to go wrong

will find yourself in a match fight that ends up on the ground. Instead, branch straight to striking using the concept of your closest weapon to his nearest target. In this case use a knee strike (or if necessary multiple knee strikes) to the outside of the thigh mass (peroneal nerve); this will allow you to secure a greater degree of compliance from your combative subject. From here, it will be quite easy to lock his arm and control his exit.

Level of force: option 3

This method is to be used with the kind of person I would consider to be a high-threat individual. Maybe they're a known troublemaker or just someone who gives you that 'Don't f**k' vibe. You will know if you meet such a person.

Personally, I wouldn't attempt a holding-type restraint in such cases. Instead, I would work from my fence and, if talking failed, would be looking at using deception in order to make him drop his guard, followed by a well-practised pre-emptive strike.

However, if I already had that individual in the off-centre position and felt that they were just too strong to restrain without a time-consuming struggle, then I would, again, strike first. As mentioned earlier, by using the come-along position you have completely opened up all their centre-line targets: jaw, throat, solar plexus and groin are all accessible to you.

(a)   (b)

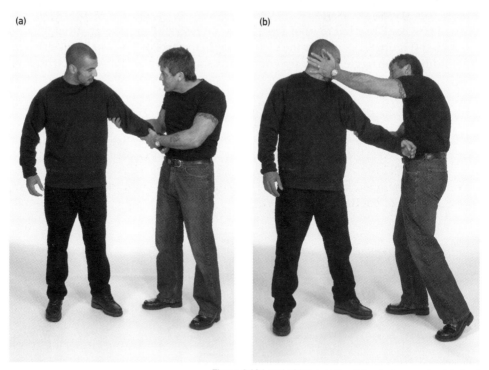

Figure 8.12 Level of force: option 3 (explosive rear hook to jaw)

A sudden sharp pull onto an explosive rear hook with the open palm heel, right on the button of the chin/jaw would do the job nicely (Figure 8.12). Remember, if the aggressor starts to become too much of a handful, and the level of threat dictates it, striking is your best option; so don't hesitate.

Arm wrench

Here we are looking at using the arm wrench, as a slight jolt to cause a distraction or in order to gain compliance. It should be used in this way rather than as a means to cause damage to the arm, so don't be overzealous with it.

(a)   (b)

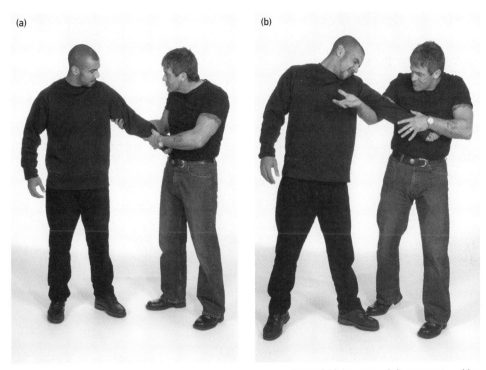

Figure 8.13 Arm wrench from escort position

To work it from the escort position, just hold the arm as described above (see Figure 8.13a). Then, as you feel resistance from the aggressor, just jerk the elbow up with the crook of your arm as you pull his hand to your body (Figure 8.13b). Use a little body mechanics behind, along with a short explosive movement. This will induce enough pain to gain compliance and allow you to continue your escort.

(a)

(b)

(c)

Figure 8.14 Arm wrench preceded by elbow shot to the bicep

This method also works well when preceded by an elbow shot to the bicep. Just make two quick snappy movements from your hips, strike the arm then wrench.

Flesh grab to escort

The flesh grab is a good method to use to get someone up off the ground quickly, particularly if you are struggling to get them out and they either fall over or deliberately drop their weight in an act of defiance. With some individuals it might be dangerous to try and lift them back to their feet, particularly if they are trying to pull you down with them.

The last place you want to be is in a grappling situation, rolling around on the ground: if this individual has mates around, it is at this point that they will start to play football with your head; someone who is not involved may even try to stick the boot in while you are down – that's the nature of society today. Lots of door staff have been bottled or stabbed while rolling around on a nightclub dance floor in this way.

In such a situation – where you are still on your feet and your combative subject is on the ground – the method described here has proved successful for me and many a door supervisor I know. All you do is slap your open hand onto an area that offers a fair degree of loose skin. A few examples include holding one arm as you slap and grab a small handful of loose flesh between the bicep and triceps area of the upper arm. Other good places include the 'love handle' area at the sides of the waist, the fleshy part at the front or back of the armpit, or (as shown in Figure 8.15) the loose, fleshy cheek area on the side of the jaw and face.

(a) 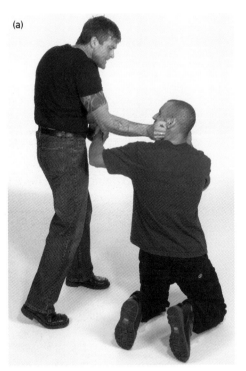 (b)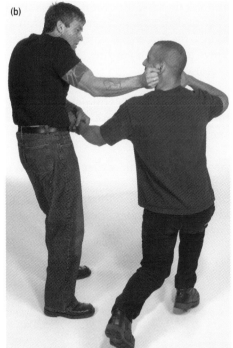

Figure 8.15 An example of the flesh grab to escort

Once you have a good grip on the skin, make sure you squeeze it tight using your fingertips, not prints. From here, use loud verbal commands such as 'Just get back on your feet and keep moving!'

If necessary, you can now drag and pull in the direction you want the individual to move (e.g. the exit) (Figure 8.16). This method is a merely a means of pain compliance that acts in more or less the same way as a volume control: you apply pain to a certain degree and keep it there; if he complies, no further pressure is added; if he doesn't, then just turn up the volume slightly.

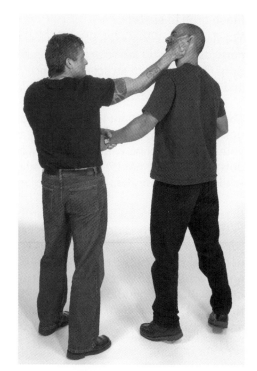

Figure 8.16 Pull in the direction you want the individual to move

Using the V control to bottle-strip

Come closing time, it is inevitable that you may have to ask the occasional patron more than once, and maybe several times, to finish up their drink. You will often find that some people will want to hang on until the very last moment. Some may even see this as a way to test your patience: you may have given them drinking-up time, asked them politely several times and then left them to drink up, yet still had to come back and ask them again. Another situation you may have to deal with is where the patron attempts to take his/her drink with them as they leave. There are laws regarding taking drinks off the premises.

If a patron is being extremely awkward, then there comes a point when you will be forced to remove the bottle/glass physically from them. The method we will look at here has proved successful time and again.

As we have seen in earlier chapters (see Section 6.4, page 58), whenever you have to deal with a potentially aggressive individual it is a good idea to use a tactile fence as you communicate. The only difference in this situation is that you are now using one hand in a kind of V shape to monitor the bottle/glass, just in case the individual attempts to use it as an improvised weapon.

In Figure 8.17 the lead hand is used, in a V shape, to monitor a bottle held in the hand of a potentially awkward customer (this could also be used with someone holding a glass).

Figure 8.17 V control used to monitor a bottle

From here, in one movement, your left hand squeezes into the meaty part of the bottle-holding thumb (being sure to use your fingertips, not prints), at the same time as you take hold of the bottle with your right hand and 'strip' it from them, pulling sharply upwards through where the fingers and thumb meet (Figure 8.18).

Figure 8.18 'Stripping' a bottle from an awkward individual

This is the weak link in the grip and the bottle will come free quite easily (Figure 8.19).

Figure 8.19 The bottle should come free easily

The sequence of photos in Figure 8.20 shows the control in application. You are talking to an awkward customer and the time has come where, in spite of numerous requests, the bottle must be taken. Work from your tactile fence using the V control to check the bottle-holding hand and using your right hand to protect the gap between you both (Figure 8.20a).

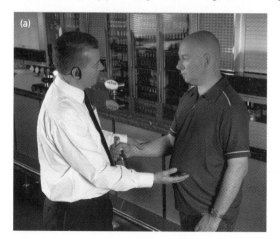

Figure 8.20 V control to bottle-stripping in action

Bring the stripping action into play as described above (Figures 8.20b and c).

Additional note

050508

The action of using the hand in a tactile way will offer you an indication of the individual's intention, which should dictate how you choose to act. Here is an example: if the person makes no attempt to pull their arm away and is behaving semi-compliantly, then take control straight away; if, however, the lightest touch is met with a show of aggression such as the individual pulling their arm away suddenly, then you will have an early indication as to their intention and restraint may become necessary.

The push/pull method

The push/pull method involves a sudden turning of your aggressor, either by using a simultaneous push or shove to one shoulder as you pull sharply on the opposite shoulder, or by quickly moving him to his off-side by pulling sharply behind his elbow and turning him that way. In both cases, you should accompany the action by moving your own body to a position behind the aggressor.

When this action is performed in one sudden explosive movement, it is extremely disorientating for the aggressor, thereby providing a means of distraction before an attempt at restraint is made. From here you could go straight for a choke hold or into a pain compliance technique.

The first push/pull method we will look at here is the nose/face control. We will then go on to look at ways of controlling the aggressor by controlling the neck/head area and controlling via the use of clothing.

The nose/face control

The sequence of photos in Figure 8.21 illustrates nose/face control. Keep your hands high as you try to de-escalate (Figure 8.21a). From here, as restraint becomes necessary, place both hands on the aggressor's face and head in one fast motion. The left hand goes to the back of his head as the right palm, flat, goes straight to the face (Figure 8.21b).

(a)

(b)

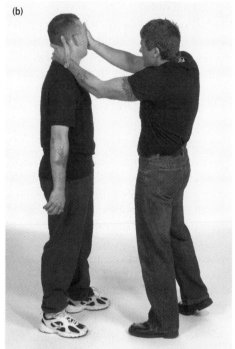

(c)

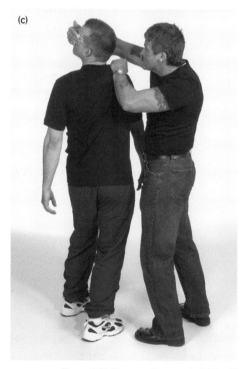

Figure 8.21 The nose/face control (step 1)

You are looking to turn and control the head by using a 'smearing' action to the side of the nose. Push the nose to the right as you control the back of the head with your left hand (Figure 8.21c). Using this anti-clockwise movement, continue the turn by pulling on his shoulder (as shown) until he has his back to you.

(a)

(b)

Figure 8.22 The nose/face control (step 2)

Keeping his head back, take his weight on the inside crook of your left elbow, as shown in Figure 8.22, and lock the head into place with your right hand. In the sequence shown in Figure 8.22, I am controlling the head via the philtrum (nose and upper lip) but you can also use the bottom of the jaw bone to lock it all in place. From here, use your man for cover and walk him backwards to the nearest exit.

Additional note

There are two points to be made here: be sure to *control* his bodyweight rather than let him just fall back on you, making him too heavy to manage – stay close to his back and as upright as you can; you may find that the aggressor starts to flail with his arms or attempts to pull at yours – just keep your head down and everything tight (ride the storm) then keep moving towards the exit (Figure 8.23).

Figure 8.23 Keep your head down, everything tight, and keep moving towards the exit

The use of neck restraints

Governing bodies such as the SIA offer no guidelines relating to control and restraint. However, there are important considerations to be borne in mind regarding the correct amount of force to be employed by the door supervisor. One such relates to the use of neck restraints. The use of such holds is usually strongly discouraged because of the significant dangers involved in using them.

Stabilising a violent aggressor's head via control of the neck is indeed a very effective method of restraint, and I speak from experience, but it must be taken into account that the throat and neck are a vital area, containing the windpipe, voice box and carotid arteries – all of which could sustain damage if too much force is applied. The throat, of course, contains the airway, and the result of constricting either the carotids or the trachea will cut off the blood and oxygen supply to the brain, causing unconsciousness in a matter of seconds.

One of the two main potential dangers is that, if you apply too much pressure directly across the windpipe, this could cause life-threatening damage. Instead I would strive to avoid this area by wrapping my arm so that my bicep and forearm lay to either side of the neck. Where possible, I would apply only enough pressure to subdue the aggressor and drag him out, rather than render him unconscious.

Herein lies the second danger. If the person becomes unconscious, the restraint must be released immediately. Most times you will find that the person will thrash around violently for a few seconds then just slump. Other times the only indication you might get is a slump in their body weight, which will feel heavy on your arms. It is at this point that they are out, and you must release the hold and, if possible, place them in the recovery position. If you keep the hold on for too long after unconsciousness there is a very real danger of brain injury or death.

Because of the dangers of the use of neck restraints, details of how to apply this method of restraint are not set out in this book.

Turn to grab and palm strike

From a fence position (Figure 8.24), use a fast push/pull to spin your opponent by pulling on his left shoulder with your right hand, as you shove his opposite shoulder with your left.

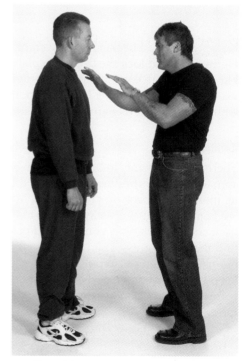

Figure 8.24 Turn to grab and palm strike (step 1)

Maintain a grip on his clothing with your right hand, keeping your arm horizontal so that the point of your right elbow now lands in the centre of his back (Figure 8.25).

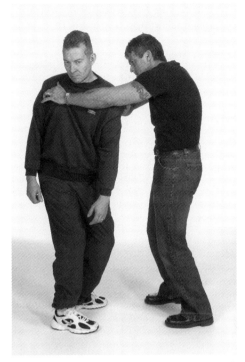

Figure 8.25 Turn to grab and palm strike (step 2)

From here, grab the scruff of his neck and 'rag' him backwards as you push with your elbow to break his structure. Drop your head and control his exit (Figure 8.26).

Figure 8.26 Turn to grab and palm strike (step 3)

From here you have the option to palm-strike the back of his head if the level of threat dictates such action (Figure 8.27).

Figure 8.27 Use a palm-strike to the back of the head if necessary

Additional note

Understand that the amount of force you use from here will depend on the level of threat. If your aggressor is showing compliance, then just shove him outside – nothing more.

The head hold

To the onlooker, this method looks as if the door person has grabbed the non-compliant aggressor in a headlock in an attempt to escort him off the premises.

From a fence position (Figure 8.28), start by putting in an incidental strike to the side of the

Figure 8.28 Head hold (step 1)

aggressor's neck with the inside edge of your forearm (Figure 8.29). This action will stun him, making him easier to control.

Figure 8.29 Head hold (step 2)

From here continue the motion into the hold (Figure 8.30) by sliding your arm around his head/facial area while stepping across the front of him with your right leg. This will bend him forwards at the waist. From here, catch hold of your right wrist with your left hand and force your right forearm bone into the side of his face, anywhere between his temple and chin.

Pull on your wrist as you force down with your body weight. Now you have a secure pain-compliance technique that you can maintain or increase as needed. From here you can walk him out or, if necessary, throw him easily over your hip.

Figure 8.30 Head hold (step 3)

8.4 Methods of intervention

Head control (A)

This is a useful method of removing one individual from another. Perhaps you need to pull one person off someone else to break up a fight, or you may need to intervene in order to protect a fellow member of staff. Approach from behind, placing your left arm around the aggressor's face just under the chin, tilting his head straight back with the inside of your elbow.

As you do this, grasp the top of his head with your right hand, being sure to place your splayed fingers on the ledge of bone just beneath the eyebrows – not in the eyes but at the top of the forehead, just above the orbital sockets (Figure 8.31).

From here, pull his head back sharply and turn your hip in towards him, so that your left buttock and hip are now in the small of his back (Figure 8.32); pull him backwards to break his posture. Now you can control his exit from the premises.

Figure 8.31 Head control (A) (step 1)

(a)

(b)

Figure 8.32 Head control (A) (step 2)

Note how your hip is turned in to your aggressor's lower back in order to break his balance and structure. Make sure that you control his body weight and don't just allow him to fall back on you. Keep his head tilted right back and escort him out (Figure 8.33). Remember: where the head goes the body must follow. It's also a good time to be heard saying something out loud like 'Just calm down and keep moving and you won't get hurt!' As mentioned before, this is useful from the point of view of third-party observation – in case you have to defend your actions later.

(a)

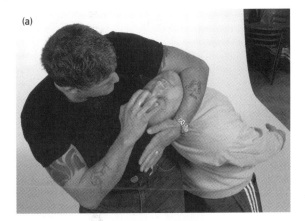

(b)

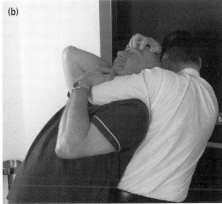

Figure 8.33 Some closer views of head control (A)

Head control (B)

This technique could be used in the same kind of intervention situation as head control (A). Approach from behind, but this time place your left hand over the aggressor's mouth, holding his chin and jaw bone (Figure 8.34a). At the same time, grab his right arm with your right hand then, in one continuous movement from the second you make contact, turn his head to the left using a quick and controlled motion (Figure 8.34b).

(a)

(b)

Figure 8.34 Head control (B) (step 1)

At the same time strive to bar his right arm across your chest by pulling hard and fast with your right hand (Figure 8.35). If you can't get the arm straight, just maintain a tight grip on his wrist and keep his arm close to your chest. From here you can escort him out of the venue, or if the situation dictates you can take him to the floor by lifting your elbow to clear his head (keeping your hand on his face throughout) then driving him straight down to the floor in one controlled motion.

Figure 8.35 Head control (B) (step 2)

This turn and control of the head is very disorientating to the aggressor, who can then be controlled off the premises by pulling him backwards. Or, as shown in Figure 8.36, you have the option to take him to the ground and control him in place with your knee by pinning it on his head. You might need to take this course of action if an aggressor has to be detained until the police arrive, or perhaps because he has stumbled over as you attempted to take him outside. In either case, maintain your position until you get assistance. This is particularly important after a show of aggression or if the subject is going to be arrested and therefore considers he has nothing to lose. Also be sure to maintain active awareness in case of further threat from additional aggressors. While he is in this position, you can monitor the aggressor's hands and pockets for weapons as shown here.

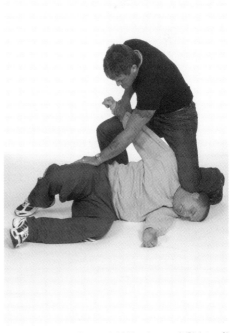

Figure 8.36 Head control (B) (step 3)

Thai kick intervention

This approach uses the pivot/Thai kick from behind as a means to intervene. This low-line kick to the thigh is a good low-level-of-force option which has proved extremely effective in this kind of situation on numerous occasions.

As a struggle ensues in the bar area, approach from a good position that offers the side of the aggressor's thigh as a target (Figure 8.37).

Figure 8.37 Thai kick intervention (step 1)

From here, just kick straight in and through the leg (Figure 8.38). See the section on the 'pivot/Thai kick', later in this chapter (page 125) for fuller description.

Figure 8.38 Thai kick intervention (step 2)

This motion will disrupt the aggressor's structure and balance, making a two-man restraint possible (Figure 8.39).

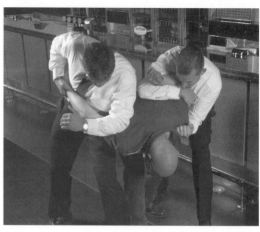

Figure 8.39 Applying a two-man restraint

From here, the door supervisors take an arm each and lock the limbs in place as described earlier (Figure 8.40). The aggressor is brought up onto his toes by the door supervisors inserting the tips of their fingers into the shoulder/pectoral cavity. From here, remain vigilant to your immediate surroundings and escort the gentleman out.

Figure 8.40 With the aggressor's arms locked in place, he can be escorted to the exit

Belt pull intervention

The belt pull is a good way to break an aggressor's balance and structure. The action of pulling one way at the waist while pushing the opposite way at the upper body will place your aggressor at a disadvantage, thus creating the opportunity to restrain. The photos in Figure 8.41 depict a scenario in the bar area: an aggressor has started to get physical with a colleague; you approach from the side/rear of the aggressor and apply the belt pull from behind.

Figure 8.41 Belt pull intervention (step 1)

One hand takes a secure hold on the back of his belt and waistband area as the other shoves high into the aggressor's upper back. Use a fast push/pull motion as you explosively pull on his waistband while shoving him forward with the other hand (Figure 8.42). From here, both door supervisors can restrain the aggressor and escort him out.

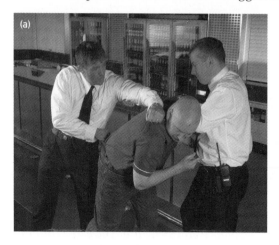
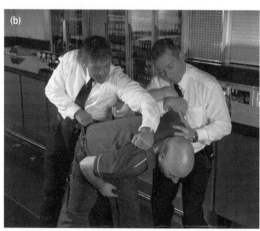

Figure 8.42 Belt pull intervention (step 2)

As shown in Figure 8.43, the belt pull can be used to both the front and back of the aggressor's belt area as a means to break their balance and get them out the door.

Figure 8.43 Belt pull intervention: variations

8.5 Group restraint

The reality of using a method of control and restraint, via holds and pain compliance, in order to control a *seriously* violent, struggling and non-compliant aggressor is a tall order for any one person, regardless of their physical ability. Just watch one of the TV reality police shows that depict violence and public disorder on the streets of Britain, and you will frequently see that it can take three to five, or more, police officers to restrain and handcuff just one combative individual. That's why the methods of individual restraint we've looked at here are usually preceded by some kind of strike or distraction.

The only way to restrain a violent individual with the lowest chance of injury to all parties concerned, with a high probability of success, is via group restraint: one subject controlled by two (or even three) individuals at one time. This is the only way that hospital orderlies and prison officers performing cell extractions will operate. Yet you as a door supervisor are expected to be able to restrain aggressive individuals using such means, and in some cases by yourself. Even then, no such training will be offered to you as part of your SIA qualification.

If all non-physical options are spent then you will have to work with what you've got, and group restraint is your best option. So always seek assistance wherever possible and use the rest of this manual as a good support system for you as an individual.

We have already covered the method depicted in Figure 8.44 as an individual restraint (see the section on the come-along restraint, followed by arm control, on pages 80–90). This can also be performed as a two-man restraint team, as shown here. Remember that restraining holds are simply physical methods used to gain control of a combative subject. Performed as a team they are designed to prevent or decrease harm to yourself and others.

Figure 8.44 The group version of the come-along restraint, followed by arm control

8.6 Pre-emptive strikes

Understand that, most of the time, if you wait for final confirmation that you're going to be assaulted, it will come in the form of injury to you.

(Kelly McCann, world-leading authority in the high-risk security industry and Close Combat fraternity)

Your personal resources include politeness, intelligence, an abundance of patience and, where absolutely necessary, a proactive physical response which manifests itself as your favoured pre-emptive strike. If your instincts tell you that the person you are dealing with is too dangerous to restrain, that an attack upon your person is imminent and this person now means you serious harm, then you may have to act first, using a pre-emptive strike. At this point you will have assessed the situation and decided that there is no other alternative than to strike first in order to prevent an attack upon your person. It is my opinion that, for door work, open-hand techniques are to be favoured, for several reasons.

- Open-hand strikes can be used effectively by men and women without risk of breaking their knuckles, as with closed-fist punching.
- A good heavy slap has massive knockout potential, sending a big shock to the central nervous system (CNS).
- From the point of view of police involvement, a slap is a lot easier to justify. It is how you slap/strike that will give your technique knockout potential.
- The pre-emptive strikes suggested here are a few of the basic ones used in the system of unarmed combatives I teach.

BE AWARE

Remember that the idea behind your pre-emptive strike is to attack your aggressor in a way that disarms his preparation to attack you. This is determined by instinct, as well as a good understanding of body language and pre-fight indicators (see Section 5.5). You must have the honest belief that you are about to be attacked in order to act pre-emptively from both a moral and legal standpoint. If this condition is present then justification is on your side.

The open-hand slap

The target area for this slap is generic; by this I mean anywhere from the top of the head to where the neck joins the shoulder. Striking the face, which can be considered a lower-level-of-force option, will send a massive shock to the CNS. The aggressor will become completely disorientated and incapable of focusing his vision due to a temporary altered state of consciousness, giving you ample opportunity to follow up or restrain if necessary. The nerve-sensitive facial area offers the less potentially injurious option.

The thing to consider here is that, in any violent situation, particularly when you are in a severely adrenalised state, most of us will find that fine targeting becomes difficult. For this reason, if you have exhausted all your options and now have to strike, then do so – and give it everything you've got.

In the example shown in Figure 8.45, the hands are first held as if talking in exclamation; the strike is then thrown from outside the aggressor's peripheral vision. The strike can also be thrown in a fast arc straight from your pocket.

(a)

(b)

Figure 8.45 The open-hand slap (variation 1)

Working from a de-escalation type of fence (this is when both hands are held high and open with the palms facing outwards – kind of subservient-looking), simply step forward with your left foot moving in the direction of the strike. As you turn, impact the face with a heavy slap, placing your full body weight behind the blow.

(a)

(b)

Figure 8.46 The open-hand slap (variation 2)

The back-hand slap

The back-hand slap is best used on a potential aggressor who is standing slightly to your flank. It works best from either the hand-on-chin position shown in Figure 8.47, or from a hands-together, in-front-of-chest position. The target area for this strike is the facial area.

Figure 8.47 Suggested starting point for the back-hand slap

To slap, giving no sign of what you are about to do, just strike straight out to the target from wherever your striking hand is. Move in the direction of the strike and whip your hips in a split second before the strike lands (Figure 8.48). This will ensure that your full body weight accompanies the strike for maximum effect.

Figure 8.48 The back-hand slap

The back-hand slap can be followed immediately by a forehand slap; the two can be used in combination for maximum effect. Performed in this way the back-hand slap is thrown first as previously described (and as illustrated in Figure 8.48), but is immediately followed by a forehand slap with the other hand, all in one smooth movement. By this I mean that, if you think of the back-hand slap as one beat and the forehand slap as a second beat, then the movement involved would be one … two. What I recommend is that the two slaps be thrown in combination, using an almost simultaneous action. In this way the second strike gathers impact power from the momentum created by the first, and is twice as effective.

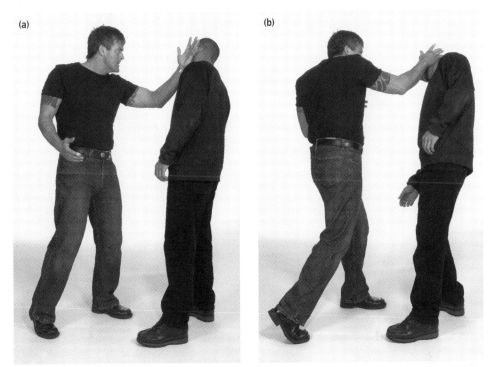

Figure 8.49 The back-hand slap can be followed by a forehand slap

With this technique, we are again looking to the facial area as our target. The impact of the slap(s) will certainly shock the CNS, but will leave the recipient relatively unharmed – other than perhaps a temporarily altered state of consciousness and a slightly red face.

The double-hand slap

This strike can be thrown from a hands-down-by-the-sides position, straight to the target, which is basically both sides of the face or neck. If you throw the strike from a fence position, you will need to cock yours hands slightly before you strike. The best way to disguise this set-up is to turn your palms out slightly as if talking in exclamation (see Figure 8.50). Then simply ask your opponent a brain-engaging question such as 'What's this about?' This will also act as a trigger for your attack, which in turn will eliminate any indecision on your part as to when to strike. This is just one way of employing artifice (deception), and is a good tactic to use with all your strikes. This kind of ploy should be bought into play when you practise your striking on impact equipment.

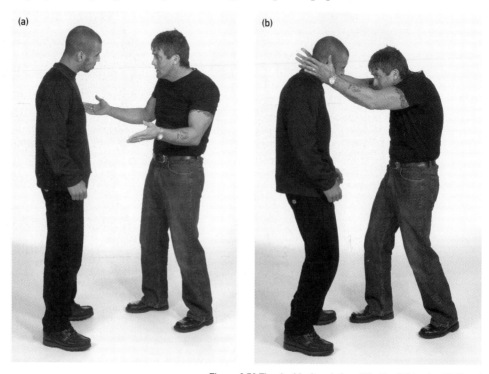

(a)   (b)

Figure 8.50 The double-hand slap: 'What's all this about?' Bang!

The double-hand slap in reaction to a grab

In a situational sense, it is important that all your open-hand strikes work for you – both reactively and as a pre-emptive action. In the example shown in Figure 8.51, the aggressor has grabbed my shirt and yanks me forward. The situation dictates that I have to *react* to this assault as the advantage of pre-emptive action has been lost. Make no mistake, an attack is on its way. A grab of this kind will usually precede either a head-butt or an attempt to slam you into something. Regardless of the aggressor's intention, your response must be immediate. In this example, I use the double-hand slap to both sides of his neck/face.

(a)

(b)

Figure 8.51 The double-hand slap in reaction to a grab

The groin slap

Again, working from a fence, you would most likely use this strike on a taller individual – why head-hunt when there is a much closer primary target available to you? If necessary, you can set up this shot by taking his attention upwards first – perhaps by shoving his head back with your lead hand. This will obstruct his field of vision and coax a reaction from him: he will be likely to raise his hands to clear the obstruction. By this time, though, your strike will already have impacted his groin. Step forward with your left foot to the outside of his right foot, moving in the direction of the strike. This allows your full body weight to accompany the slap. As you move, your rear (striking) hand makes a small circular motion as it sweeps in towards the groin, to add momentum to the strike. Close and check his arms as you impact the groin with your slap. From here restraint is possible.

(a)

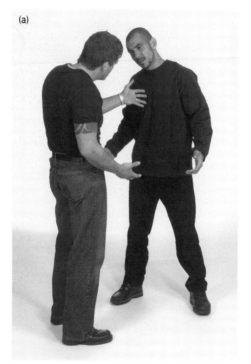

(b)

Figure 8.52 The groin slap

Palm heel strike

This is a piston-like strike, employing the heel of your palm of your strong-side rear hand. The target area is anywhere on the face or head. As long as you can hit hard, you will get a good – literally stunning – result. Just take a step forward and fire the palm straight to the target (as shown in Figure 8.53). Make sure you avoid making any kind of signal of intent that would give the game away, such as pulling your hand back before you strike or tensing up your face. Just stay relaxed and strike explosively from where your hands are. This can then be followed up by closing in on your aggressor, in order to place him in a position of restraint, using which he can be evicted from the premises.

(a)

(b)

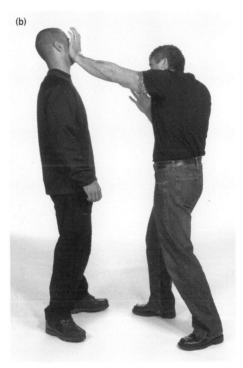

Figure 8.53 Pre-emptive palm heel strike

This strike can also be used in reaction to a single-handed, grab and punch threat (Figure 8.54). Just pin the aggressor's holding hand to your chest with one hand as you simultaneously strike with the other. Remember: from the grab, his attack will quickly follow, so make your response immediate.

(a)

(b)

Figure 8.54 Reactive palm heel strike

Forearm strike

This strike is performed with the radial bone of the forearm while keeping the arm slightly bent. The strike is thrown straight from the hip to the side of your aggressor's neck. This was a favourite pre-emptive strike of veteran ex-doorman and self-protection instructor Jamie O'Keefe. He likes to call it the 'invisible baseball bat'. As you strike, drop your body weight and move in the direction of the strike with a twist of hip commitment (Figure 8.55).

(a)

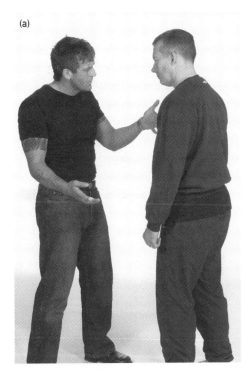

(b)

Figure 8.55 Forearm strike: the 'invisible baseball bat'

Keep your fence hand out and throw the strike straight from your pocket in a short, non-telegraphic arc straight to the junction between the neck and the shoulder (this area is known as the brachial plexus). Note that it is the radial edge of the forearm bone that is used for striking (Figure 8.56).

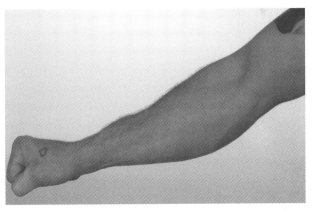

Figure 8.56 Strike with the radial edge of the forearm bone

Elbow strike

The elbow can be used from a variety of angles to a variety of target areas. As a pre-emptive strike, however, we will stick with just one simple method of delivery. The elbow is basically a close-quarter weapon, and target areas for the elbow really depend on the level of threat you are dealing with. For our purposes, we must strive to stay within the confines of reasonable force, so the two examples given below have that aim in mind. The elbow strike is probably the most potentially damaging strike technique you can use; for this reason, you should avoid targeting the head unless this is a last resort. A full-on strike to the chest, shoulder or bicep area of the upper arm can have a great disabling effect and completely shut down one side of your assailant's body.

In the example in Figure 8.57, the elbow strike is applied to the upper arm preceding an arm lock restraint (as described on pages 82–83). In all cases when using the elbow, make sure that the strike is delivered using the tip of the elbow point and not the forearm. Get your full body weight behind the strike by vigorously twisting your hips a split second before impact.

(a)

(b)

Figure 8.57 Elbow strike to the upper arm

In the scenario depicted in Figure 8.58a we are at close quarters, using the fence in a tactile way (e.g. both hands are in contact with the aggressor's body). From here you should pull the aggressor's arm towards you, as you fire a simultaneous elbow strike to his chest and shoulder area (Figure 8.58b). Such a shot delivered with the point of the elbow and a fair degree of impact will temporarily incapacitate that side of the aggressor's body, leaving you in an ideal position to restrain and escort him out.

(a)   (b)

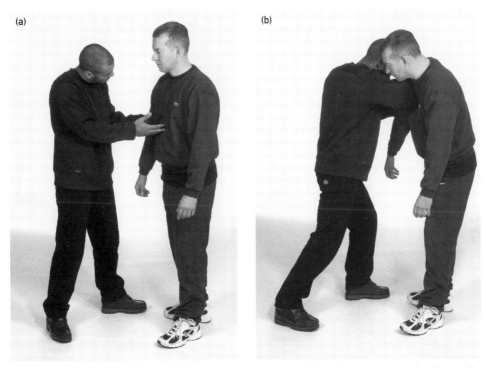

Figure 8.58 Close quarters with tactile fence, followed by elbow strike

Spike elbow

This is a great tool to use if someone throws any kind of angular attack or if an awkward individual simply attempts to encroach on your space. All you do is, from a fence position, step in with a falling drop-step action and spike him in the chest area with the point of your elbow (see Figure 8.59).

(a)   (b)

Figure 8.59 The spike elbow

This is exactly the same action we would use for a 'flinch' response in as much as the head is dropped, but you are still keeping your aggressor in view as your hands come up to protect your face and neck. The spike elbow arm is bought up high into the centre line and your opposite hand is open and in front of your face as a monitor.

In Figure 8.60 we see the strike in application. In order to ward off a forward-moving aggressive encroachment, drop your head and body weight forward and spike the aggressor in the centre of their body mass with the point of your elbow.

Figure 8.60 The spike elbow used to ward off an aggressive encroachment

BE AWARE

Remember that the final precursor to violence will be your aggressor's attempt to take down your fence and close the gap. This is your pre-attack cue to spike in with your elbow. In this way you are attacking your opponent's preparation to attack, thus acting pre-emptively. As with the palm heel strike, the same method can be used reactively against any swinging kind of attack, making you offensively defensive.

Knee strike

If the person you are trying to restrain starts to prove a little too problematic to handle, then one good low-level-of-force option you could use is the knee strike to the outer thigh area (peroneal nerve) of your potential aggressor. Another good target option is the groin, but basically anywhere on the low-line area will work effectively as long as you use the point of the knee and strike with a fair degree of impact. If the situation warrants it and the opportunity presents itself for a quick knee strike to the groin as your initial pre-emptive attack, then seize the opportunity to land this fight-stopping shot without hesitation.

This strike works best from a very close-range position, such as a clinch. One method is to grab hold of the back of the aggressor's neck (as shown in Figure 8.61) then fire the knee or multiple strikes into the thighs and/or groin. This scenario depicts a knee strike to the groin from a Thai-boxing style neck clinch. This is just one way to employ its use. Throughout this book you will see the knee used in a variety of situations. Ensure that you get a good grasp of how to use this very functional close-quarter tool.

(a)

(b)

Figure 8.61 Knee strike from a close-range position

Figure 8.62 shows another example, striking the inner area of the thigh from a side-on struggle.

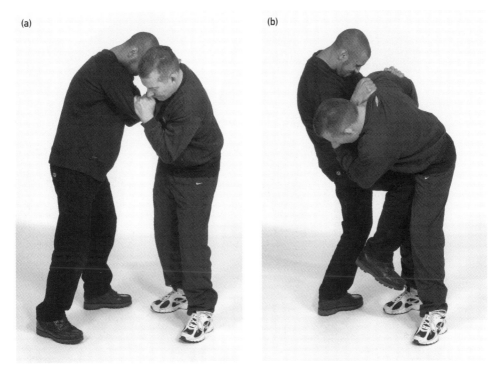

(a)   (b)

Figure 8.62 Knee strike from a Thai-boxing style neck clinch

Pivot/Thai kick

The pivot, or Thai, kick is basically a 'roundhouse' (i.e. sweeping round) kick performed with a semi-straight leg. Impact is made to the outside of the thigh muscle (peroneal nerve) with your shin bone, just as in a Thai kick. The finish position should leave the foot of your kicking leg with the heel higher than your toes. This can be achieved only by pivoting on your support foot and committing your hips through the strike. Think of your leg as a heavy log that you are going to swing through the target without retraction.

Working from a fence position, shove your aggressor hard in the centre of his chest with the flat of your hand (Figure 8.63). This will create space by making him take a sudden step backwards, leaving his lead leg exposed to the pivot kick.

(a)

(b)

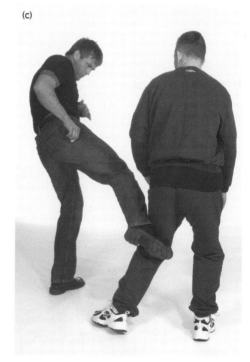

(c)

Figure 8.63 Pivot/Thai kick

This is a good low-level-of-force option that has worked well for me in the past. The kick will take away the aggressor's mobility and give him a major dead leg, but he should be relatively injury-free apart from that. I also like the fact that, with this strike, the person will usually fall laterally onto one shoulder, avoiding impact to their head as they hit the ground. This alone makes it a safer option. With mobility gone the person should be easier to control: as the saying goes, 'If he can't stand, he can't fight.'

8.7 Dealing with common physical attacks

This section deals with the 'What if?' factor, as in 'What if I'm caught unawares and have to react to some kind of attack from an aggressor (be it a grab or a sucker punch)?' This is what is called 'situational practice'. The thing to understand from the off is that if you find yourself in a situation where you have to react to something your opponent does to you, this means that you are at a disadvantage. The plain fact is that action will always beat reaction and a pre-emptive response will always remain the better option if avoidance is not possible.

The fact that you are now in a situation where you have to react indicates that you have been caught off-guard and at a low level of awareness, in which case any assault on your person will be classed as an ambush attack. In such a scenario, the saying 'How you train is how you will fight' definitely applies. That's why it is essential that you address such situations in your training. In order to keep things simple – simple being the only thing that works in a 'live' situation – we are going to deal with a variety of the most common primary attacks that an untrained aggressor is likely to use.

You don't need to bog yourself down in a huge variety of defences as there are only really a few practical possibilities. The first of these is the classic 'haymaker' or 'big right hand' angular punching attack. Most people are right-handed, although you should also train for the left-handed attack. The thing to understand is that, although this is a common method of punching, it is the line or angle of attack that we are concerned with, regardless of whether the attack itself is a punch or the hand is holding a weapon such as a bottle. The angle in this case is the same.

Then we need to take into account what's known as 'Hick's law'. This refers to the number of choices you have and how they affect your response time. If you practise four or five different responses to one particular attack, then, when the time comes to put your response into action, there will be a significant time delay as your brain attempts to select the required response to fit the situation. This lost time could make all the difference. Hick's law dictates that if you have just one well-trained response to a particular stimulus then your response time will be almost instant. If you increase your choices to two then your response time will increase slightly. Add several more choices, and in the time of need you are likely to experience indecision and time delay, or what self-protection guru Peter Consterdine terms 'log jam'. So, to keep things as simple as possible, we are going to look at no more than two responses to each situation, making both adaptable should the need arise.

The cross-arm cover

Figure 8.64 shows the arm and body position for the cross-arm cover. The head and body weight are dropped forward as the left arm crosses in front of the face/head and the right arm crosses in front of the throat/chest area. This cross-arm position offers maximum protection to your head and neck as both forearms and the points of both elbows drive forward into the aggressor's upper chest area. (This can be used as a pre-emptive action or as offensive defence.)

In application, this technique is used as follows: as you perceive your aggressor's intent, drop your centre of gravity and drive through him with the cross-arm cover. Should the level of threat warrant such a response, you can follow this up with knee strikes to his low line.

The example in the sequence of photos in Figure 8.65 shows how the cross-arm cover can be used against a bottle attack. As the bottle comes in (how switched on you are will depend on how much reaction time you have), cover your head and drop straight in with your elbows; you are aiming to get right inside the arc of the weapon and drive into the aggressor's body. From here, form a clinch and strike with the knee. Strive literally to blow out his base.

Figure 8.64 The cross-arm cover

(a)

(b)

(c)

Figure 8.65 Cross-arm cover, followed by clinch and knee strike

The cover and fend

The cover and fend position is achieved by placing both palms on the crown of your head, leaving your forearms and elbows covering your face and chin. This position is never static but constantly moving – covering the entire head/facial area rather like an exaggerated motion of washing your hair – as you sway your body and move your head to the left and right, to present a harder-to-hit moving target.

Figure 8.66 The cover and fend

The hands should move constantly, in order to protect the head and face from a multiple punching attack. The front of your forearms and elbows deal with any straight frontal punches, while the sides of either outer arm can be closed tight to cover any angular (hook-line) punches from the side. In reality you want to close him down after one or two punches are taken on the arms, and finish it from the clinch.

TRAINING TIP

A good way to practise is to have a training partner, wearing boxing gloves, throw multiple punches at your head as you stand with your back to a wall. It is important to go forward only as you cover and fend – moving back gives your opponent room to operate and develop power. By training with your back to a wall, the only way you can go is forward. Practise the drill for, say, 20 seconds then close him down into a clinch. This will help you to develop the composure necessary to deal with this kind of multiple punching attack. In a real-life situation, though, you should go for the close-down as soon as the attack starts.

Whether you are fending multiple punches from a skilled boxer or a windmilling Neanderthal, the response is the same. Cover your head with your hands and arms, presenting your opponent with only the points of your elbows and forearms to hit and drive forward to close him down as soon as the assault starts (Figure 8.67).

(a) (b)

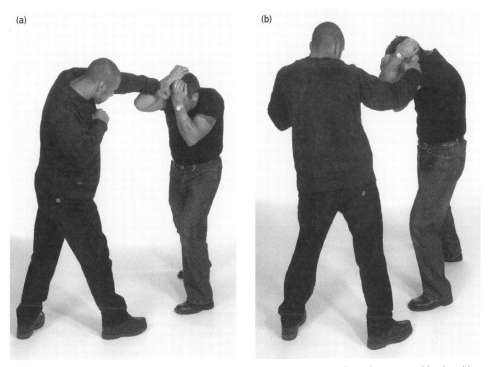

Figure 8.67 Closing down an aggressor from the cover and fend position

As the aggressor continues to throw punches, strive to destroy his fists with your pointed elbows as you dive through his space and guard, and clinch onto his neck (Figure 8.68).

Figure 8.68 Drive through the aggressor's space to clinch onto his neck

From here, move in to finish with multiple knee strikes to the groin and thighs (Figure 8.69). Follow up as appropriate.

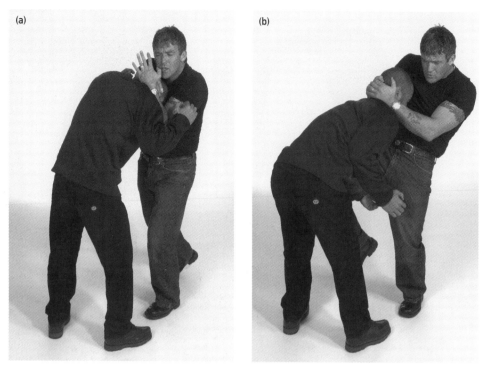

Figure 8.69 Finish with multiple knee strikes to the groin and thighs

Dealing with a head lock

The main point to bear in mind here is that as soon as an aggressor has you in this kind of hold a couple of imminent possibilities exist. The first is that while holding on with one arm the aggressor's other hand will be punching at your face. The second is that the aggressor may have grabbed you in this way with the intention of taking you to the ground. In either and all cases, your response must be practised to the point where it is both instantaneous and aggressive.

As shown in the sequence of photos in Figure 8.70, situations such as that illustrated require that you go straight for the groin slap. As you do so, keep your other hand busy by reaching up and over the aggressor's head until your index and middle fingers find their position under his nose (on the philtrum).

(a)

(b)

(c)

(d)

Figure 8.70 Dealing with a head lock

Once there, pull his head back in one quick movement in order to break his balance and structure as well as expose his chin for an open-palm strike, which will quickly bring an end to the situation.

8.8 Using your environment

Where necessary, certain aspects of your environment could, and should, be used as a means to control an aggressor. A bar stool, for example, can come in very useful to create a barrier between you and a broken beer glass in the hands of an aggressor with bad intentions – not forgetting of course the strike potential of the chair or stool should the desperate need arise. Some additional environmental factors to consider are as follows.

- What is the floor surface like? Is it slippery?
- Are there any tripping hazards nearby that might cause you to stumble and fall during an altercation?

When observing your environment, where possible try to position yourself with your back to a wall so that any approach on your person will by necessity be frontal. This applies tenfold if you are dealing with more than one aggressive individual. The ideal is to be in a position where you can physically deal with one person and still keep anyone else who may decide to get involved in plain view and at bay. In a multiple-assailant situation your environment can be the deciding factor. If you can position yourself so that you can deal with one at a time, you will take away their ability to attack all at once. This will give you a good chance as long as you act pre-emptively and back-up is on the way. If not and your life is in danger, then you will have to protect yourself with all-out committed aggression and literally blitz whoever's in reach. In such a situation it's time to get big or go home.

If you stand at the top of a stairwell, for example, this would make it very difficult for anyone to approach you from any angle other than the front. Placing yourself just inside a doorway will also allow you a degree of control over the angles. If it all kicks off on the door and you can get the door closed and locked, then do so. If not, then stand your ground just inside the entrance so that any approach will have to be frontal, thereby limiting any attack from your flanks. Again blitz anything that moves and hope that back-up is on its way.

Another thing to remember is, if there is no staff toilet in your venue and you have to use the customer facilities, always use a cubicle and ensure the door is locked. Don't use the urinal, where you'll have your back to Joe Public and a low level of visual awareness.

The methods described in this section illustrate various ways in which you could utilise your immediate environment – such as walls, door jambs, doors. In some situations you might use a door, table or bar stool to create a barrier. You might use your positioning to the doors and walls as a means of cover. You might even apply such aspects of your environment as a way to achieve leverage and compliance in a potential aggressor. It is important to take these ideas on board and add them to your armoury.

Using a wall

In the scenario depicted in Figure 8.71, my colleague is struggling with an aggressor and blows are about to be exchanged. From here my priority is to assist my colleague before things escalate further. I approach the aggressor from the side/rear and begin my intervention by grabbing hold of his attire and pulling him back slightly, in order to break his balance. I continue the motion, making use of the momentum I've created by shoving him into the wall. From here compliance is achieved and restraint made possible.

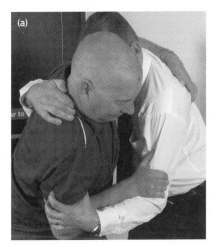

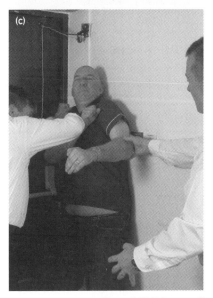

Figure 8.71 Using a wall

Using a door jamb

Here I have escorted a completely non-compliant and aggressive individual to the rear fire exit door. Sometimes you might find that getting the individual to the door is easier than getting him out of it. In the example illustrated in Figure 8.72, the patron has decided to struggle and is holding on to the door jamb as his demeanour starts to become a lot more combative. Rather than struggle with him and risk possible physical assault, I decide to maintain my grip on him and utilise my environment. In this case I shove him backwards into the door jamb (using just a jolt as I monitor the impact). This creates enough of a distraction for me to get him out of the exit.

Figure 8.72 Using a door jamb

Using a door as a barrier

Any good door person will tell you that it is a lot more sensible to deal with potentially troublesome patrons on the front door than it is to take a chance and let them in, only to be called to an incident later on inside the club. Once they're in, you will have to find them and possibly struggle to get them out again. The job of standing on the front door is usually reserved for the more experienced door supervisor; most head doormen will usually be appointed here. As well as representing yourself, your employer and the venue with the utmost professionalism while on the front door, another of your duties is to act as a filter system: you are there to keep out the violent minority.

Any known troublemakers, previously-barred patrons or individuals displaying unacceptable behaviour should be stopped right there, at the front door. In addition, getting the main door closed and locked in a hurry has proved to be a saving grace for many a door team, particularly if you are outnumbered and the odds are stacked against you. In situations like this bravado has no part to play – this is pure self-preservation, so make use of this aspect of your environment, get the front door shut and locked and call for back up. End of story.

Figure 8.73 Using the door as a barrier

In the scenario illustrated in Figure 8.73, a situation has erupted into violence on the front door. We've got two extremely aggressive individuals attempting to force entry and a few more *en route* to help them out. Here an attempt is made to get the heavy front door shut. If necessary, the door will be used on either aggressor as an impact weapon, as will the door jamb. This photo also shows how one door supervisor's radio can be employed as an improvised impact weapon, striking one of the aggressor's hands to clear his grip on the door.

BE AWARE

Although this point has already been mentioned, it bears repeating. Placing yourself just inside a doorway will allow you a degree of control over the angles. If it all kicks off on the door and you can get it closed and locked then do so. If not, stand your ground just inside the entrance so that any approach will have to be frontal, thereby limiting any attack from your flanks. This kind of situation may present dire, even life-threatening, consequences to you and/or your colleagues, so blitz anything that moves and hope that back-up is on its way.

Using the edge of the bar

In the scenario illustrated in Figure 8.74, I am using the edge of the bar as a means to gain compliance of a combative subject who has attempted to rugby-tackle me to the ground. I have grabbed hold of his attire and redirected his forward pressure into the edge of the bar. From here I will attempt to restrain him and control his exit.

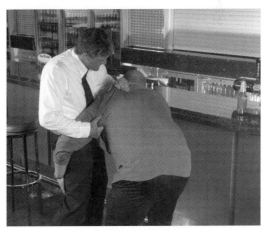

Figure 8.74 Using the edge of the bar

BE AWARE

Please understand that I am by no means suggesting that part of your job description as a door supervisor involves bashing non-compliant customers into walls, tables and bar edges in order to gain compliance. What I am suggesting is that your level of force must, where possible, mirror the level of threat you face. If a situation is about to become violent then your priority, first and foremost, is self-preservation, and this is followed by the safety of your colleagues and customers.

If, taking a hypothetical example, I plan to try to remove an aggressive patron from the bar area, I will always take someone with me for back-up. Then, working as a team, we will endeavour to remove the troublesome patron with the minimum force required for the task at hand. Let's say, for argument's sake, the individual has several friends in the immediate area, all equally as 'up for it' as he is and, before I can do anything else, I find myself being grabbed and in a struggle with an extremely aggressive and dangerous individual.

One possible consequence of such a struggle may involve me going to the ground with this man, where three of his friends will eagerly take part in using my head as a football. (I know of three doormen who have been kicked and stamped senseless in this way, one of whom was permanently disabled and will spend the rest of his life in a wheelchair because of it.)

One of my friends, Geoff Thompson (the veteran ex-doorman from Coventry), had several friends who also worked the doors and were fatally stabbed in such an affray. So, make no mistake about it, if I can prevent this kind of escalation in violence by simply ramming an individual into any object that might help take the wind out of his sails, then that's exactly what I would do.

Remember, though, the physical options offered here are all merely suggestions born out of real-life experience. My job is to educate you to the possible consequences of some of the violent situations you may come across, and to show you some of the successful options that have proved consistently useful for me and my peers in the past. Where possible, door staff should always seek the non-physical response but the sad reality is that some people will see your kindness or politeness as weakness, and will be only too eager to leave you injured or worse. In such situations you need to use all your resources to stay in one piece.

CHAPTER NINE

WEAPONS

9.1 Improvised weapons

There are many everyday items that can be used as makeshift, or improvised, weapons should the need arise. One specific item I would like to focus on here is the pen.

The pen

As I've already mentioned, all door staff should carry a small notebook and pen for recording events and incidents in any case – but the pen in particular can come in very handy if used in the way described here. The thing about the pen is that it is not a weapon by design, nor has it been converted or adapted in any way to be used as such. For civilian self-protection I teach access and deployment of a pen as an improvised weapon in a variety of ways, none of which are suitable for use on the door or in a book such as this.

That is, all except one method. This was shown to me some time ago by self-protection guru, Jamie O'Keefe. The pen is held in what Jamie calls a 'cigarette lighter' grip (see Figure 9.1). Held in this way the pen can be used to trap and pinch small amounts of skin at locations such as the back of the arm, the love handle area (just below the waist) and, in some cases, the ear lobe, in such a way as to achieve pain compliance.

Examples of this method's uses include escorting a non-compliant individual from a seated position (Figure 9.2a) by using the pen grip on the ear lobe in order to lift him up from his seat. Or, from the side, a come-along position using the pen to grip a small fold of skin, taken from behind the triceps area (Figure 9.2b and c). As a low-level method of pain compliance, this can be very effective. In all cases, though, make sure that you couple your actions with a verbal command such as 'Just keep moving and we'll have no problem!'

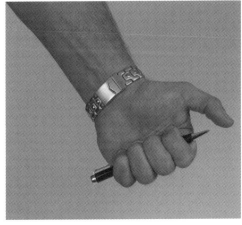

Figure 9.1 A pen held in the 'cigarette lighter' grip

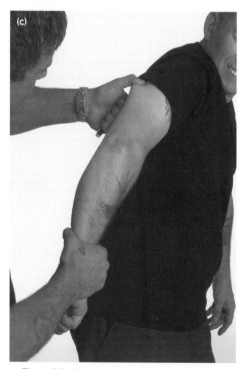

Figure 9.2 Using a pen to achieve pain compliance

The chair/bar stool

Use of a chair or bar stool in order to create a barrier, and an equaliser against a bottle or an edged weapon, can prove effective for buying you a little time until back-up arrives – not to mention the fact that it can also be used as an impact weapon should such a last-resort need arise. Remember: if someone pulls a knife, or breaks a glass or bottle to threaten you (a not-too-uncommon occurrence these days,) then you have been offered deadly force by your potential attacker. The beer bottle is one of the most immediate weapons of the pub and nightclub environment, along with the beer glass and the heavy glass ashtray. All of these are capable of being used as both edged and impact weapons, with frightening results. In my time working within the door-security environment I have seen some of the horrendous injuries that broken glass can inflict. With this in mind, you must understand that, in such a situation, all bets are off and you must do whatever it takes to deal with it.

In Figure 9.3 I am using a chair in order to create a barrier between me and my aggressor's knife. Note how the chair has been turned at an angle, so that the top and bottom legs line up with his throat and groin. This increases my target option efficiency should I need to strike out with the chair. As always, this action is backed up with a firm, loud verbal boundary such as 'Stay where you are! Drop the knife!' This will alert everyone in the immediate area to the fact that a potentially lethal assault is in progress and back-up is needed.

(a)
(b)

Figure 9.3 Using a chair as a barrier

Figure 9.4 shows one of my colleagues fending off a bottle attack with a bar stool. In this case the bottle is being used as an impact weapon. In such situations you should, again, use loud verbal commands, telling the aggressor to 'Stay back!' Don't back yourself into a corner; if necessary show that you have the intention to strike with your makeshift barrier. As with the chair example, it is a good idea to angle the legs of the stool so that they line up with the aggressor's throat and shoulders.

Figure 9.4 Using a bar stool as a barrier

BE AWARE

A broken bottle, or the jagged spears of a broken beer glass, in the hand of someone with bad intentions, is quite literally offering you deadly force. Just imagine such an item rammed into someone's throat or jugular and you'll get the picture.

9.2 Offensive weapons

It is very important that all door supervisors are aware of the dangers of offensive weapons, and understand the laws relating to them. Any door team must seek to employ effective search procedures (see Section 2.5) in an effort to monitor and reduce the likelihood of such dangerous articles being brought into the premises. Apart from any breach of law, weapons present obvious dangers to door supervisors, who are required to evict unruly patrons and intervene in fights. That danger lies in the fact that any offensive weapon that has been smuggled into the venue could be turned against door staff as they attempt to do their jobs. The logic is simple: the fewer weapons that get through, the less chance there is of this happening.

Any item that is considered a weapon by design, or that has been adapted in any way to be used as such, will fall into the category of offensive weapon. Although there are many people who may use screwdrivers, Stanley knives or similar articles in their line of work, there is simply no reasonable explanation that would give them cause to bring such an item into your premises, and such items should be considered equally offensive.

In July 1996 legislation was passed in the form of the Offensive Weapons Act. This came about as a result of the increase in the illegal use of weapons, making both the carrying of offensive weapons in a public place and having articles with blades or points in a public place arrestable offensives. This means that anyone, including a door supervisor, who finds a suspect in the act of committing such an offence, or who has reasonable grounds for suspecting them can now make an arrest (see Section 2.6).

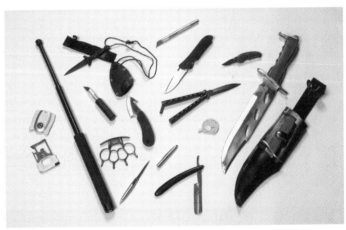

Figure 9.5 Some examples of offensive weapons

Definition of an offensive weapon

An offensive weapon is defined as 'any article by design, or adapted for use, for causing injury to any person, or intended by the person having it with him for such use by him or some other person'. We'll now look at several examples.

By design

This relates to any article made from the outset for the purpose of combat. Such items include swords, knives, bayonets, knuckle-dusters, expandable batons and similar items. In addition, we can include any chemical irritant such as Mace (usually supplied in an aerosol), CS gas and OC pepper spray.

Adapted

This category includes everyday items that have been changed in some way to make them more offensive in nature, such as makeshift edged weapons. These might be things like a razor blade melted into a toothbrush, a sharpened belt buckle, a metal bar with a taped handle, or – more common to the nightclub environment – a beer bottle, glass or glass ashtray that has been smashed deliberately in order to produce a cutting weapon.

Intended

Here we are looking at items that are considered inoffensive if employed for their intended use, but that are made offensive by the user's intention to cause physical harm with them. Examples could include basically any item that could be held in the hand and used to strike with, with the premeditated intention of causing injury.

Seizure

In the course of your duties you will inevitably have to seize items such as those described above from customers, either at the point of entry during a search procedure or from inside the premises should such possession come to light. In such a situation it is vital that you do not keep the item in question in your possession for any longer than is absolutely necessary (policies may differ according to the situation and your venue's criteria for dealing with such situations).

In all cases, such items should be handed in to the head doorman or someone from your management team. If the person found in possession is to be arrested and handed over to the police, then the weapon will be handed over as evidence at the same time. If it is decided to confiscate a weapon and just refuse entry or evict the customer, then whoever takes possession of the weapon should log this in the venue's incident book and lock the item away securely until such time as it can safely be destroyed or handed over to the police.

BE AWARE

The law applies equally to the door supervisor as it does to any member of the general public. The courts do not look kindly on anyone employed within the security industry found in possession of an offensive weapon. Therefore under no circumstances should door supervisors be allowed to carry or use such items during the course of their duties.

9.3 Edged weapon awareness

Before we start on this subject, I feel that there is a need to discuss certain aspects relating to the knife issue as it stands in the UK today. From a personal point of view – and speaking both as a self-protection/defensive tactics instructor as well as a time-served doorman – I would like to delve a lot deeper into this subject. Although we are not generally thought of as a knife-carrying culture – as compared to, say, the Philippines, Indonesia or certain states of the USA – statistics show that the majority of street crime that takes place in this country involves some kind of edged weapon. It is therefore necessary to assume that, in any potentially confrontational situation, there is a good chance that your assailant will be carrying a weapon.

There are plenty of laws that aim to keep tight control of people walking the streets with knives and other weapons. Articles such as switchblades, flick knives, butterfly knives, push daggers, belt-knuckle knives, sword canes and knuckle-duster knives are all banned from sale, yet such items are regularly found during routine searches. Apart from the items mentioned above, any individual 18 years or older can legally obtain cutting weapons of horrendous design from a vast array of outlets.

Banning the sale of such items is a step in the right direction, as are the occasional knife amnesties that the police offer every few years (these are periods during which individuals are given the opportunity to place any and all such items into a sealed box, outside any police station in the country, no questions asked). However, neither of these measures will ever eliminate the problem – simply because the problem lies in the individual's *intention* to cause harm; it is nothing to do with the tool employed as a weapon. Without intention, a weapon is merely a tool; with applied intention, however, any individual can cause lethal injury – even armed with an apparently innocent pencil.

This being the case, I feel that the penalties for those involved in knife crime need to be more severe. However, until that time comes and the statistics start to improve, we need to become more informed. When I say 'we', I mean anyone concerned with their own self-protection and personal security, as well as that of their family. This is especially important for those working within the field of door security.

The law relating to carrying knives in the UK

The Criminal Justice Act 1988 states that you may carry a knife with a blade length of up to three inches as long as it is capable of folding. Since then, the Knives Act 1997 has come into force – it is the most recent anti-knife law and effectively bans the sale of any knife suitable for combat. Last year alone, there were 272 reported deaths in the UK resulting from knife wounds. The current penalties in place for possession of an edged weapon range from a £50 fine to up to four years' imprisonment.

Some examples of edged weapons

As we have seen, practically any object that has a point and/or a sharp edge can be employed as a slashing/stabbing tool. This, added to ill intention, equals a dangerous weapon. The following list gives some examples of such items – some are designed for combat, some for utility, others are simple everyday items that could be improvised for ill intent with little or no makeshift engineering:

- screwdriver, chisel etc.
- broken glass
- ripped piece of tin
- ceramics
- Stanley knife/blade
- pencil/pen/metal pen refill
- syringe
- bicycle spoke.

Other examples include, obviously, *any* knife by design. The list is practically endless: as long as an individual has the intention to cut or stab there will always be an edged weapon available.

If we take a look at the history of early edged weapons we can see how man is a tool-bearing animal. Our first weapon was a simple stone. Stone-Age man then realised through experience that certain-shaped stones (i.e. those with sharper edges) could do a more efficient job. Moving on, he realised that if he bashed one rock against another, he could create these sharp edges and points, and hence the first edged weapons and tools were born. Next came the Bronze Age, then the Iron Age, followed by man's ability to melt steel … and the rest, as they say, is history.

9.4 Counter-weapons training

Counter-weapons training is a major topic and deserving of an entire book on its own if justice is to be done to it. Please bear in mind that no one system of martial arts or combatives will ever have all the answers in terms of how to use empty hands against weapons, particularly where knives are concerned. The methods I teach are based on what I feel are the best approaches I have come across during the past 24 years of my training. They are based on an array of methods and practical experience from Filipino kali and western combatives, as well as on the experience I have gained from the four live knife situations I have been involved in to date.

For simplicity, any cutting tool – regardless of whether it is a Stanley knife, stiletto blade, broken glass or a beer bottle – will be referred to from here on as an 'edged weapon'. Any of the above-mentioned tools can really only be used against you in either a swinging or slashing motion, or they can be jabbed and poked at you in a stabbing motion aiming at a number of targets on your person. Therefore, if a knife has been drawn and you have seen it, then the most probable attack will now be some kind of slash or stab. I will not cover counter-measures to such attacks here as space will not allow me to do the subject justice, but we will take a look at a couple of methods that can be used to deal with the weapon before it has been drawn.

Body-language cues

We have already seen how important it is to be able to rely on our awareness, our instincts and our understanding of body language. We have discussed certain elements of this in preceding chapters (e.g. Section 5.5) – for example, understanding the verbal and physical cues of aggressive body language, and also the *modus operandi* of our potential aggressor's attack ritual and dialogue. We are going to need to become more specific here, however, in terms of picking up on any indication that our potential assailant is carrying a weapon. Spotting any clue to this fact before the weapon is bought into play may well be the only thing that gives you the chance to take the action needed to get the jump on the situation. If your aggressor already has a weapon to hand and the intention to use it, then you will most certainly have a harder time dealing with the problem than if your instincts had told you that he was carrying and you took action as soon as he tried to access the weapon. This would have enabled you to shut down the threat before he could get the knife out.

Remember, if you find yourself in a confrontational situation, always assume that the aggressor is armed. Always scan for their hands. Can you see both hands and all his fingers? Some of the most common methods of concealment are 'palming' the knife (holding it out of sight against the palm when the top of the hand is uppermost), holding it flat against the thigh or keeping the carrying hand concealed in a pocket or behind the back, out of view. So look out for concealment: if you can't see your assailant's hand(s), or if his palm is turned in flat against his leg or concealed in a pocket, ask yourself why. Remember, too, that you could be approached with some kind of distracting dialogue in order to divert your attention before the aggressor draws his weapon. Watch out for erratic eye movement. Is his face pale? Are his eyes wide? Does his body shiver? These are all indications of adrenal reaction and are likely to be present if his intention is to stab or slash you. Such indications may be the only factors that separate you from dealing with the threat and maybe meeting your maker.

We will now look at a couple of drills that will enable you to practise working from these body-language cues, in order to shut your aggressor down quickly and clinically. Several examples of body-language cues are shown in Figure 9.6. The first (Figure 9.6a) shows the aggressor move one hand behind his back. The second (Figure 9.6b) shows one hand concealed by clothing – in this case placed inside the aggressor's coat. The third (Figure 9.6c) shows one hand reaching into the front of the waistband, obscured by the aggressor's T-shirt, as the other hand attempts to clear the garment for access.

(a)   (b)   (c)

Figure 9.6 Examples of body-language cues

Trap-and-strike drill 1

In practising this drill you will be working from the reactions or body-language cues given off by your training partner. Face each other at arm's length, making sure that you keep your arms by your sides and are standing in a neutral position with no fence. Your partner will have a training knife behind his back, tucked into his waistband. Start at no more than 50 per cent speed and have your partner slightly exaggerate his movements so that you get an idea of what you are looking for.

Basically, if he starts to turn away slightly by moving the shoulder of his weapon-bearing side, this is your cue to move. If one of his hands starts to move behind his back or slightly out of view, then that too is a cue to move. You are looking for any sign that tells you that your partner is reaching for a weapon. Your immediate action should be to step forward (see Figure 9.7) to shut him down and break his balance, while seizing the arm that is moving by grabbing it at the crook of the elbow and jamming it tight against his body (see Figure 9.8).

Figure 9.7 As the aggressor starts to move, step in immediately

As you do this, your free hand goes straight to his face for a chin-jab or a face-smash strike, or (the more common reaction) straight to his throat for a claw-grip larynx grab. From here you continue with forward pressure and continuous strikes to eliminate the threat (again see Figure 9.8).

Once you both have an understanding of the drill, forget about compliance and have your partner move at full speed and make a committed attempt to draw the training weapon and thrust it towards your body. If he touches you with it you would have been stabbed. This is likely to make you a little jumpy, but that's a good thing and it's how you need to be to produce the most effective reaction.

When you've got to grips with the basics, you can start bringing in some role-play and have your partner wear body armour so that you can administer strikes against them with a degree of realism. You should also practise with your partner wearing a heavy jacket, so that all you know is that he will draw the knife from somewhere. This could be from a pocket, under his shirt on the front of his waistband, strapped somewhere on his back or even to a limb, or anywhere else he can think of. Any and all methods of concealment have been used and all are fair game to try out in this drill. Once you have practised this drill a few times you will see just how dangerous the edged-weapon threat can be. Stopping attempted weapons-use at this point is your best chance of dealing with the threat, as once the knife is out it is much harder to deal with.

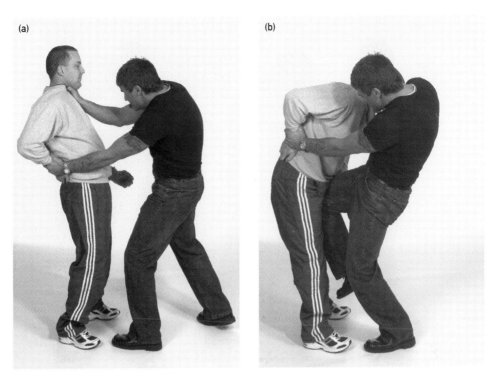

Figure 9.8 Trap his arm to the side of his body. Be sure to make a simultaneous grab for his throat, making sure that you break his balance with forward pressure; think of replacing his footsteps with your own as you follow up with continuous strikes – in this case knees work really well

Figure 9.9 Trap-and-strike drill 2 (step 1)

Trap-and-strike drill 2

In the scenario shown in Figure 9.9, the aggressor has the knife concealed in the front of his waistband, under his T-shirt. As soon as a motion is made towards the weapon, you should drop-step forward and pin both the aggressor's hands in place to his body.

Continue this forward motion by driving the top of your head straight into his face. Follow this up by walking violently through him with a rapid knee-strike to the groin (Figure 9.10).

Figure 9.10 Trap-and-strike drill 2 (step 2)

CHAPTER TEN

THE PSYCHOLOGY OF CONFLICT MANAGEMENT

10.1 The 'fight or flight' response

How 'fight or flight' works (SIA definition)

If we are seriously threatened, our bodies prepare us for 'fight or flight' action by releasing adrenalin. When adrenalin is in the body, it makes the heart pump blood more quickly into the large muscles. Our eyes open wide to take in as much information as possible and focus on the threat. Our hearing also starts to shut down, and the performance of fine and complex physical skills is seriously reduced. Overall our body is geared up for fight or flight action. This involves either running away (flight) or standing our ground (fight). This reaction is a natural animal instinct, which man has had since prehistoric times, and it has helped us to survive. In modern times the dangers we face are different, but we still instinctively respond this way when we feel threatened.

Choosing to fight

We can influence whether another person decides to run away or stay and fight. We increase the chances of someone choosing to fight when we:

- invade their personal space
- continue to make them feel threatened
- block their exit path.

10.2 Understanding how anger leads to violence

Anger has a similar effect on people as fear. The body is 'geared up' for action. Frustration leads to anger, anger leads to aggression and aggression leads to violence.

Frustration → Anger → Violence

Figure 10.1 How frustration leads to violence

Author's note

I consider the effect that adrenal stress can have on operational performance to be a very important subject. An in-depth understanding of this topic is essential if you are ever going to learn how to control it and operate effectively. As with other areas that I have mentioned, I think the SIA's training package should cover this subject in more detail. For this reason, in the section that follows I will attempt to give you as in-depth a discussion as my experience and learning will allow.

10.3 Understanding fear and the survival stress response

Fear is your best friend and your worst enemy. Control it and win.

(Anon)

In times of danger each and every one of us will feel the effects of the survival stress response (SSR). (There is more on the SSR in Section 10.4.) This is triggered into action via the security control centre of the brain, which is called the 'amygdala'. The amygdala is basically the brain's threat-detecting organ.

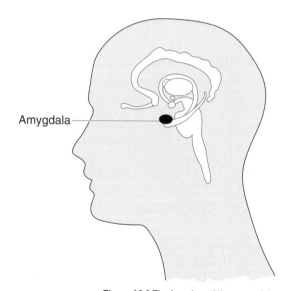

Figure 10.2 The location of the amygdala

During times of stress, such as a violent confrontation, the 'sympathetic nervous system' takes over and a neural surge will cause an increase in heart rate that will in turn raise your blood pressure. This results in blood being withdrawn from your extremities in order to be pumped to your vital inner organs. Blood is also drawn from the brain cortex for the same reason. The result of this is that your thinking is impaired – in particular your decision-making abilities. Due to this restriction in blood flow to the brain, the neo-cortex, or higher brain, is non-functional, and the limbic system, which is the part of the brain that is responsible for emotions, will take prominence, rendering all complex decision-making impossible.

The result of this is that your intelligence is now reduced to that of a dog. In addition, you will also experience what is known as 'adrenal dump'. This will create a release of endorphins that will make you stronger, faster, and more resistant to pain and shock. The flip-side of this is the mental implications that also have to be dealt with. These include auditory exclusion, or impaired hearing, and tunnel vision (where your peripheral vision closes down, hence the need to scan actively), among various other effects.

For a door supervisor, the most important aspect when dealing with any potentially violent confrontation is his/her understanding of the fight or flight response. Your ability to cope with adrenal stress when a situation kicks off will make all the difference to how you handle it. Ask any door person who has had their share of experience of this and they will all tell you that it's a major factor.

This being the case I find it hard to believe that the official SIA Level 2 National Certificate manual covers this aspect only very briefly over two very short paragraphs, when it should be an in-depth topic that each and every door supervisor should be familiar with and understand. The fact is that knowledge is power, and if you understand what is happening to your own body under the effects of adrenal stress then you are more likely to be able to gain control over yourself and the situation, and will be less likely to freeze up or overreact. When the body responds to danger by secreting adrenalin (the fight or flight response), this is what we often interpret as fear. If you do not understand this simple fact, then what you are likely to encounter, especially if you are startled, is the 'freeze' response. The only way to lessen the effect of this startle reflex, and prevent freezing up, is through awareness (being switched on), good threat-assessment abilities and an anticipation of the adrenalin sensation.

Because it's so important to have a good understanding of the effects of adrenalin release, we will now look in a little more detail at the things I have summarised above.

Expectation

First of all, expect to be scared. No matter how experienced you are, that is how you will feel. Fear is the natural feeling prior to confrontation and, as noted above, man has had this hard-wired instinct since prehistoric times. It is, and always will be, essential to survival. When a situation kicks off, the feeling that you would rather be anywhere else in the world other than where you are at that moment is one that is common to all. If you feel like crapping yourself, just be aware that you are not on your own: we all (without exception) feel fear – it is the natural product of adrenal release.

Knowledge and understanding

You must learn to understand 'why' and 'what' is going on inside yourself when you are faced with danger – in your case, as a door supervisor, the danger of an aggressive and violent confrontation. If you have this understanding then you will be better prepared to move past the mental and physical sensations of adrenalin release so that physically you can function effectively.

Side-effects of adrenalin

Expect to get a fluttery feeling in your stomach, even a little nausea. This is the body's way of helping you to eliminate any excess weight you may be carrying from an earlier meal, in order to allow you to move faster and more efficiently. It is also why you may feel the need to urinate or empty your bowels. You may also start to sweat, and your heart rate will increase.

Another common symptom is shaky legs. Some get this worse than others. This happens as a result of the adrenalin surging through the bloodstream at high speed. A loss of skin colour may also occur. This is nature's way of protecting you: the blood leaves the surface of the skin so that you will bleed less should you get cut. It is also because the blood is being pumped to your vital organs (e.g. the heart and lungs), where it is needed most.

Your ability to use your usual thought processes will become less rational, making all decision-making a lot more difficult. This is due to blood leaving the brain to be put to use elsewhere. Your eyes will become wide and staring in an attempt to take in more information; this is due to the effect of tunnel vision, which will make your field of vision rather like the view you would see if you were looking through a toilet roll tube. If you are focused on a threat in front of you in this way, this can make you vulnerable to an attack from the side, so try to keep your peripheral vision open by looking around you often. Your hearing will also become impaired due to what is known as 'auditory exclusion', in an attempt to tune in to the threat.

Your ability to perform fine motor skills or complex actions will become seriously reduced, leaving you with only gross motor ability. On the positive side, adrenalin will make you stronger, faster and more resistant to pain.

As you can see, all these effects have a purpose and are in fact essential to our survival. Do try to gain an understanding of adrenalin and its effects, so that you can use it to your advantage.

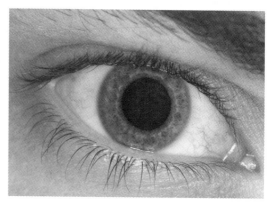

Figure 10.3 This man has an enlarged pupil, a side-effect of an adrenalin surge

10.4 Coping with sensations

Desensitisation

Desensitisation is a very strange feeling of which most people have little experience. However, it is through desensitisation that people whose jobs put them in harm's way on a regular basis (firemen, police officers and security people like door staff and bodyguards) become better able to deal with the effects of adrenalin. This is due to the fact that the repeated exposure to situations that cause adrenal release gradually desensitise them to its intensity. The main reason individuals can act in the face of danger is because they anticipate and expect these feelings of fear. When you have experienced them before and know they will occur again under similar circumstances you will not be caught off-guard. This is why you need to expect and accept the effects of adrenalin, as noted above: they will *always* be present in any confrontational situation in which you may find yourself. These feelings will *never* go away and are essential to your survival.

With understanding and regular exposure you can therefore become very capable of using adrenalin to your advantage and in a way that helps you function effectively. You must first control your inner self by taking deep breaths and relaxing your shoulders. Slow your body movements down so that you don't look guarded or jumpy. Your demeanour should be natural, smooth and controlled. This does not mean you should not use an aggressive approach – in some cases strong, assertive communication can be effective – but if you stay cool the subject may doubt his ability to fluster you and question whether he has chosen the right person to attack. He may wonder why you are so calm and imagine you have back-up or are more of a veteran at this game than he is.

The survival stress response and your heart rate

Scientific research into the adrenal state – also referred to as the survival stress response (SSR) – carried out by a scientist in this field called Bruce Siddle, has indicated that our ability to function under the effects of adrenal stress is directly related to an increase in our heart rate. At 115 beats per minute (bpm) most people will start to lose fine motor function. This means that, as mentioned above, skills that involve hand–eye co-ordination or finger dexterity will become difficult to perform.

As the heart rate increases to 145 bpm and beyond, your body will start to reduce the efficiency of certain bodily functions that it considers to be less essential to your survival during this time of stress. This might include, as noted, effects to both your visual and auditory system, as well as temporary impairment to certain areas of the brain. The thing to remember is that, in combat, your heart rate can go from 70 bpm to 220 bpm in less than a second. Such a case can trigger a state of 'hyper-vigilance', or the dreaded freeze response. At the very least your decision-making abilities will be severely impaired.

Further research by Siddle suggests that the ideal heart rate for a functional combative response allowing maximum reaction time and maintenance of gross motor skills will fall in the range between 115 and 145 bpm. The key lies in your ability to remain within this ideal range. This can be attained through certain training drills that will allow you to desensitise yourself to the effects of adrenalin. Aggression-therapy drills, simulation and scenario training in a controlled environment, using body armour, role-play and aggressive dialogue can take you a long way towards desensitisation to the effects of adrenalin, and will help develop your ability to remain relatively calm in such situations, thereby reducing the increase in your heart rate.

Breathing control

Something else that will aid desensitisation is your ability to control your breathing. In stressful situations, such as a potentially violent confrontation, there is a tendency to take shallow breaths in, followed by holding your breath or continuing to breathe in a shallow fashion, both of which serve only to increase the anxiety of your situation. Instead you should aim to feed your lungs with oxygen by breathing in through your nose, taking the air deep down into your lower abdomen and holding it briefly before expelling the breath out through your mouth. Of course, ideally you need to make such a practice both habitual and natural-looking in order to appear in complete control.

It is easiest to bring breathing control into play during the 'verbal interview' part of a confrontation or if you have some kind of pre-warning that a situation is developing (thanks to good awareness). This will give you the chance to gain control over your breathing. A helpful practice when you find yourself becoming adrenalised, or even slightly agitated, is to take three deep breaths: for each one, breathe in for three seconds, hold for three seconds and breathe out for three seconds, repeating until you achieve a calmer and more controlled state.

I used to use this method while working on the door. Whenever I was called to a situation over the radio I would use this technique en route to the scene. The lower you can keep your heart rate, the more control you will have. Although the adrenal conditioning developed through the proper use of simulation and scenario-type training drills can help you desensitise yourself to the effects of this essential biochemistry, it can never completely duplicate them to the same degree of intensity as that found in a real life-or-death situation. Such training will, however, allow you to reduce the reality gap between the dojo and the street.

You should learn all that you can about the workings of fear and adrenalin, and understand the importance of breathing control as a way of helping to lower the heart rate. However, proper desensitisation can take place only as a result of repeated exposure to these feelings. This is in line with what I said earlier, about people working in high-risk jobs who learn to control themselves and function under pressure due to the repeated exposure their working environment offers them on a daily basis. You would be amazed at what you can get used to.

PART THREE
ESSENTIAL ADVICE AND EQUIPMENT

CHAPTER ELEVEN

EQUIPMENT

11.1 Closed-circuit television (CCTV)

There are some definite pros and cons that come with the use of closed-circuit television (CCTV). Most venues will have multiple cameras covering all the main areas: bar, dancefloor, fire exits, main doors and so on. These could be linked to a split-screen monitor showing all areas, which is usually kept in the office area. CCTV can act as a deterrent to some troublemaking individuals, and will improve the overall security of the premises. Of course, all incidents recorded on tape can also be produced as evidence in a court of law – and that's where the pros and cons come in.

CCTV can help prevent the *minority* of heavy-handed doormen getting away with regular overzealous methods, as well as show when door staff had no other choice but to get physical and hands-on – assuming, of course, they had already tried to talk the situation down, or had at least appeared non-aggressive at the start and didn't just 'steam in'. That said, if a fight has kicked off, it may, as we have seen, be necessary to go straight in with the physical.

It can be a Catch-22 situation. For instance, none of the places I've worked in has had an audio link-up to the recorded events. So in situations where you've had no other choice than to be pre-emptive, it may appear to the viewer that you overreacted. Even if an aggressor has just told you that he's going to rearrange your features with a beer glass, it could end up in court with your word against his as there will be no audio proof of this. Despite this, and as I've said before, in this sort of situation you shouldn't think twice: your safety is your priority, so trust your instincts every time.

Figure 11.1 CCTV is an essential part of a venue's security equipment

In spite of this, I consider CCTV essential and I wouldn't feel comfortable working without it.

11.2 Communication equipment

Communication is another important part of door work. If you are working on your own inside and a situation suddenly kicks off, it would be nice to know that you can easily call for back-up.

Radio link-ups

At the very least you should all have radio link-up facilities so that everyone can keep in contact. It is also important that everyone is conversant with all emergency message procedures and any code words in use. For example, if a member of staff spots a violent situation developing by the bar, he/she might get on the radio and alert colleagues to a 'code amber' in the bar area. This would allow security staff to get into position in case the situation escalates. If it does, or if a fight has already started, then this might be labelled 'code red'.

These are just a couple of examples; there are, of course, others. Just make sure that everyone in your door team is familiar with your venue's practice and understands the terms and codes being used.

Earpieces

The use of earpieces has also become very popular. There are some obvious pros and cons to this: they do indeed improve communication performance and allow you to keep your hands free, but one possible flaw is that, in a fight situation, an earpiece could easily be ripped out and they are quite costly to replace. On a more serious note, if you get punched in the ear you could end up picking out bits of plastic from your ear canal for the next three weeks. That said, I still think they are an essential bit of kit. Radio link-up with the use of an earpiece is the preferred method of communication.

Other communications equipment

I have used other pieces of equipment for communication, such as a vibrating pager kept on your belt or in your pocket. This beeps and sends you simple text messages, such as 'urgent – bar area' or 'urgent – dancefloor'.

One method that was popular in the early 1980s was a system that used different-coloured bulbs above the main door. Each colour corresponds to a different area of the club and is hooked up to a buzzer (usually positioned with the DJ and behind the bar) . This method was pretty cheap to install and is still very functional.

Figure 11.2 An example of the sort of communication equipment you might use

11.3 Clothing and accessories

Most employers will expect you to wear a uniform of some sort. This will most likely be the traditional 'black and whites': black shoes (or, better still, lace-up ankle-high boots), black trousers with a white shirt, and a straight tie or dickie bow (make sure you only ever wear the quick-release clip-on variety, unless you want to end up getting strangled with your own tie). A black jacket completes the uniform. This could be anything from a blazer or a long trenchcoat to a bomber jacket with 'Security' plastered over the back of it.

Some places are a little more low-key and will require you to wear something more casual, like black jeans and a polo shirt or a hideously brightly coloured T-shirt with a 'Security' logo on it. This is common attire for event security, such as sporting or music and concert events. Apart from your in-date door badge, radio and standard-issue earpiece, there are a few additional personal items that could be considered very useful. Cushion insoles for your footwear are well worth considering – if you think about how much time you spend on your feet, you're likely to be glad of the additional comfort.

The following items may or may not come in useful, depending on the kind of establishment you're working at.

- **Steel-toe-cap boots** can prove to be an excellent equaliser – smart-looking and discreet are best.
- **A gum shield** can come in very handy in a brawl situation where punches are coming in from all directions. Keep one handy and put it in on the way to the scene. The two advantages of carrying a gum shield are, first, the excellent protection offered to your teeth should someone land a lucky punch and, second, the fact that the act of nonchalantly putting a gum shield in your mouth prior to a fight can be psychologically intimidating to your opponent.

CHAPTER TWELVE

ADVICE

12.1 Some dos and don'ts of door work

The following list of dos and don'ts aims to offer you some suggestions for dealing with potentially aggressive people. This, in turn, should help with the de-escalation process, thereby preventing a situation from developing into physical violence. Dealing with aggression is the main theme here, but we will also go on to look at various other aspects of door work in terms of situations you are likely to come across and, where possible, I will offer you some guidelines that will give you the best chance of success in dealing with them. The majority of these suggestions are the fruits of the hard-earned experience of people who have actually made them work for them time and time again, but I will also add input from the SIA where relevant.

Dos

- Do maximise your powers of observation by making them habitual.
- Do make early interventions as you observe situations develop.
- Do protect your personal space with a natural, non-aggressive stance, hands open and held higher than those of your aggressor.
- Do use relaxed and non-aggressive body language.
- Do speak in a calm but firm tone of voice.
- Do ensure that you understand the relevant laws, and the policies of your workplace.
- Do stress your own position, as well as that of your company, from a legal point of view.
- Do convey that you have an understanding of the situation, by trying to find the source of the person's agitation.
- Do try to employ your powers of verbal de-escalation.
- Do use slow, calming and deliberate body movements.
- Do control your own emotions, and breathe slowly and deeply.
- Do control your tone of voice – use it to calm and to try to achieve a rapport.
- Do set yourself a time limit on the verbal confrontation; when it is reached, be assertive and end it.
- Do give the aggressor plenty of space and, where possible, allow them an honourable escape route.
- Do employ your physical options only as a last resort.

Don'ts

- Don't show any signs of aggression – you are a professional, so act like one.

- Don't be judgemental or use any insulting or detrimental remarks.
- Don't make any threats.
- Don't be patronising or condescending.
- Don't bark orders at people.
- Don't show a lack of interest by acting inattentively.
- Don't show any outward signs of intimidation or fear.
- Don't invade anyone's personal space.
- Don't respond to taunts or personal insults; a situation will only become personal if you make it so, so try to desensitise yourself from your own personal hot-spots.
- Don't allow an aggressor to play the crowd; isolate him from the group (see the information on loop-holing in Section 7.4).
- Don't turn your back on an aggressor at any time during a confrontation.
- Don't be surprised if the situation escalates into violence in a heartbeat – always be prepared.

The above points summarise most of the things we have been talking about throughout this book. They are not listed in any particular order of importance – for many, their relevance will depend on the situation. For this reason, *all* of this information should be taken into account and put into practice. The object of these guidelines is to increase your safety as a door supervisor when dealing with aggression, while allowing you to present yourself with a degree of professionalism.

12.2 Dealing with specific situations

This section offers some suggestions for dealing with certain specific situations. As you will see, it is a good idea to absorb as much information and experience as you can, then add logic and try to formulate plans of action that can be used to deal with the situations that might occur. Write down and discuss your ideas with other members of your team, then visualise successful applications for dealing with such events. This kind of habitual practice goes a long way towards making you more efficient as a door supervisor – try using it for some of the following examples.

Defusing an argument between two parties

In a club scenario where two individuals or groups have a grievance with each other, it is always a good idea for you and a colleague to separate both parties before attempting to defuse the situation verbally. Once you have created space between them, you and your colleague can deal with each group or individual separately and attempt to control the situation effectively.

If a situation has developed, and you try to sort it out with both parties present and within sight and earshot of each other, then the job of defusing and containing it will be much more difficult. This method of 'separate and divide' is exactly what the police use. It enables you to get each person's side of the story, without the other chiming in and causing an escalation.

If you work as a two-man team then you will find this method a useful one to put into action. If, however, you find yourself working alone (never ideal under any circumstances) then you will have to take just one of the parties aside, again out of sight and earshot of the other, and attempt to defuse things that way.

The most important thing is that as a door supervisor you should never be tempted to take the side of either party. During the verbal stage of a potential confrontation, most individuals will want you to listen to, and take as gospel, their side of the story. In all cases you must strive to remain totally unbiased and professional. It's the only way you will get anywhere in such a situation. If one side feels that the security staff are taking the side of the other, they may consider that they have nothing to lose and kick off regardless.

Where possible, try to respond in an attentive and non-threatening manner, and keep your tone of voice calm but firm, while giving each individual or group the impression that you are interested in getting to the source of their agitation (see the information on verbal dissuasion in Section 7.4).

Putting such game plans together should be a team effort under the direction of your head of security. If no such measures exist in your venue, then try suggesting them. If this is met with a negative response from your co-workers then find yourself another venue to work at – I wouldn't call what you have a team. Failing that, the best you can do is to make such preparation available to you as an individual.

Dealing with an accident

In the event of an accident where a customer has been injured, the venue's manager should be informed immediately. First aiders should be on hand at the scene, accompanied by two members of security and, where possible, witnesses should also be present. Depending on the seriousness and nature of the accident, an ambulance may be called. After the event, all details relating to the incident must be logged in the venue's accident book.

Even if an ambulance is not required, you should still follow the same guidelines (i.e. inform the manager, attend the scene with first aiders, in front of witnesses). From this point, advise the customer to go to hospital for a check-up and write up the accident log book. In both examples, you will not only have done the right thing, you will also have complied with procedure and covered all the angles. If a customer is taken ill and none of these measures is met and no appropriate action taken, your venue may be liable.

Refusing entry to a customer

This scenario and the next are always potential catalysts for violence, so how you deal with them will make a great difference to the outcome. Remember, on no grounds can refusal of entry be based on race, gender or sexuality. In all cases of refusing entry, always strive to be polite and fully explain your reason(s) for refusal. There is an array of reasons for refusing a customer entry – the following list offers just a few examples.

- The venue is already full to capacity.
- The person shows indications of being under the influence of drink and or drugs.
- The person may be underage.
- The person does not conform to the venue's dress code.
- The person is unable to pay the entrance fee.

- The person refuses to be searched.
- The person is found in possession of a weapon or drugs.
- The person is banned or under an exclusion order.

Refusal scenario

To take one example, let's say that a person does not conform to your venue's dress code. The customer is met with a polite refusal and informed of your venue's policy on dress which is fully explained. If this is the only cause you have for refusal, then you should add something like, 'If you have any way of going home to get changed, then when you return I will be happy to let you straight in. Just come to the front of the queue and see me.' When explained and dealt with in this way, you have acted reasonably and will find that most people will be fine with that. If, however, in spite this, the person starts to argue and refuses to leave, then you must inform them that they are now trespassing. If this continues despite all your efforts to be reasonable, then the customer will have to be removed using reasonable force and the police may have to be called. After the event, write up a report in your venue's incident book.

Evicting a customer from the premises

There are many reasons why a customer may have to be evicted from your venue. In the majority of cases, unless violence is already in progress, the person will be asked to leave of his/her own accord and, where possible, all non-physical solutions will be pursued until such a point as reasonable physical force is the only the option remaining. The SIA guidelines include the following advice.

- Eject a customer for being suspected of theft, criminal damage, assault or carrying drugs inside the venue (where no police action is required). Some customers will leave when asked to do so, others will argue and/or may become aggressive.
- Eject a customer who breaches licensing laws by becoming very drunk or argumentative or aggressive inside the venue. Some customers will leave when asked, others will argue and/or become aggressive.
- Eject a customer for breaching a house rule such as repeatedly dancing on tables or carrying bottles/glasses on the dancefloor.

Figure 12.1 A busy dancefloor is no place for bottles and glasses

Additional variables within this area include:

- first-aid situations
- undertaking an arrest of a customer for an arrestable offence
- failing to adhere to drinking-up times
- domestic disputes

- other disputes (customers vs bar staff, aggressive complaints about service etc.)
- arguments/fights.

Incidents inside the venue

Most incidents of violence that take place inside a venue will usually result in some, if not all, of the parties involved being evicted. Here is one such example, along with suggestions about how to deal with it.

Evicting scenario

A fight has broken out inside the venue. This has been assessed quickly and back-up called in by a member of the security team at the scene. The response team is *en route* and, when it arrives, quickly assesses the situation. Front men deal with the incident as back men observe and act as back-up. The customer(s) involved is/are evicted in a controlled manner, using whatever reasonable force is necessary. Of course, this is the ideal, but if you have a good team that operates well together then this is how it can and should be done.

You can add to this an infinite number of variables that may change the situation in some way, but if you adhere to the basic principles, such as good observation before rushing in, calling for back-up, and working as a team with all backs observed and covered, then there should be minimal escalation in violence. As ever, it will be necessary to write up an incident report.

Contact and cover (SIA model)

This is a simple, well-tested and safe control system, which is used by police officers around the world. It is useful in situations where there is clearly a higher level of risk. It avoids the feeling of 'ganging up' where two door staff move together towards an individual. It is based on effective teamwork and provides a way of exercising control of a situation without it being intimidating.

The 'cover' person stands away from his colleague and the aggressive person. The 'contact' member of staff is closest to the customer and engages in any conversation needed to deal with the situation. The 'cover' staff member stands further away and slightly to the side of the customer (but still at an operational range) and keeps out of the conversation. The exact 'cover' position will vary depending on the environment, but the key point is that the 'contact' and 'cover' are each in a position to watch the other's back. The 'cover' is responsible for:

- observing the customer's reactions
- being aware of the other persons and potential threats
- watching the 'contact's' back
- being a good witness
- communication with other staff.

Game plans

Try to develop pre-thought-out plans of action (game plans) for certain scenarios. These will provide you and your team with an array of basic adaptable procedures that will give you some direction in such situations, as an alternative to trying to operate under such circumstances, under stress and with no direction. Based on what you have learned, try to formulate some kind of game plan for the following scenarios. Get some workable ideas down on paper and discuss them with other members of your team.

- There's a fire
- A customer is found with illegal substances
- A woman has been sexually assaulted
- A customer has been glassed
- A knife is pulled on a member of staff
- A suspect package is found
- A customer lets in a group of non-paying friends via a fire exit
- Someone is caught stealing purses from the cloakroom
- You are challenged to a match fight
- A customer refuses to be searched
- A fight kicks off between two large groups of people
- A customer is found unconscious in the toilets

Evaluating and learning (SIA advice)

The idea of learning from what has happened is critical at individual, team and industry level. An important aspect of learning from what has happened is to be able to record events accurately. If you do this, you will be able to reflect on the incident and think about what you did well and how you might be able to improve things next time. It also means that you can account for the actions you took. Finally, it means you can share good practice and help your organisation to learn from the incident.

Individual learning (SIA advice)

As a professional, you should continuously be recognising the things you do well in situations of conflict, and the things you might be able to do better if a similar incident occurs. You can review how you approached an incident using the following questions as a framework.

- What happened?
- Why did I react that way?
- What did the team or I do well?
- What did the team or I not handle so well?
- Why did things go wrong?
- How can I improve things if this happens again?

Feed information back to your organisation and try to look for long-term solutions to problem areas. In particular, try to identify any problems that seem to recur. This could mean that a procedure, policy or rule is not reasonable or effective. In such a case your management might want to change their rules. If confusion over entry conditions has caused continual problems you should discuss this with your manager and draw up a written policy to ensure that all parties are clear on what is expected.

BE AWARE

You may not be able to account for the actions of the sort of undermining managers who attempt to adapt the rules and guidelines as it suits them. There might be information about a particular individual or group of people who has or have been identified as particularly difficult or threatening. You could also include effective ways you have found of solving particular problems.

Here is one simple example. In situations that involve a breach of dress code it is a good idea to display a sign that clearly indicates the dress code that applies at your venue. Such a simple action can save a great deal of unnecessary aggravation.

There is more on dealing with typical scenarios in the following chapter.

CHAPTER THIRTEEN

SCENARIOS

13.1 How would you deal with these situations?

The following scenarios depict typical examples of some of the situations you are likely to experience on the door. You will be offered multiple-choice solutions for dealing with each situation. Bear in mind that there are an infinite number of variables that may change the outcome of a situation. This means that no one answer may be the solution to the problem *all of the time*. What I aim to offer is general guidance on dealing with each situation, along with one or two alternative approaches that would be considered less than ideal. Your objective is to select what you would consider to be your best option in terms of de-escalating the problem while maintaining professionalism. You will find the suggested answers at the end of this chapter.

The SIA exam

When taking the exam that leads to the SIA licensing qualification, you will be asked to answer similar questions, although the procedure will usually involving watching a brief scenario acted out on DVD. For further information on past papers and the exam itself please contact:

- **Level 2 BTEC Award in Door Supervision:** Edexcel, One90 High Holborn, London WC1V 7BH Tel: 0870 240 9800 Email: security@edexcel.org.uk
- **Level 2 National Certificate for Door Supervisors:** British Institute of Innkeeping (BII), Wessex House, 80 Park Street, Camberley, Surrey GU15 3PT Tel: 01276 684449 Email: doorsupervisors@bii.org
- **NOCN Level 2 Award in Door Supervision:** National Open College Network (NOCN), 9 St James Court, Friar Gate, Derby DE1 1BT Tel: 01332 268080 Email: nocn@nocn.org.uk

Scenario 1: refusing a customer entry

A male customer joins a busy queue seeking entry to your venue. You notice from his body language and demeanour that he is slightly intoxicated, and instincts tell you that with a few more drinks inside him he would become well and truly drunk and a probable liability.

Do you:

a) wait until the man gets to the front door before telling him that you feel he has had too much to drink and therefore won't be coming in tonight?

b) let him in regardless of his apparent condition?

c) approach the man discreetly, and politely tell him that you can see that he has had too much to drink, and therefore will not be coming in tonight, but you thought you would save him the wait of queuing up, and that he is welcome back on another evening when he appears a little more sober?

Scenario 2: incident inside the venue

From your designated point of duty you are the first to observe the start of a domestic dispute between two people inside the venue. Body-language cues indicate that the situation is about to become physical.

Do you:

a) go straight to the scene by yourself and intervene?

b) 'call in' the incident via communications and request assistance; then, along with your colleague, strive to separate both parties in an attempt to de-escalate the situation, after which you assess what action needs to be taken next?

c) wait until the dispute turns into a physical confrontation and then call it in?

Scenario 3: evicting a customer

A customer has been extremely loud and abusive to a member of bar staff after a dispute over the change he was given. You attend the scene with a colleague and make an attempt to defuse the situation. You strive to employ principles from the 'Open PALMS' and 'REACT' models, but are met with hostility and physical threats. It appears that the situation is about to escalate, and the threat of an actual physical assault to one or both door supervisors is imminent.

Do you:

a) along with your colleague, act as front men and deal with the incident by means of physical restraint, as further members of your team observe and act as back-up; after which the customer is evicted in a controlled manner using whatever reasonable force is necessary?

b) leave the subject alone in the hope that he will cool off?

c) jump on him mob-handed and get him out any way you can?

Figure 13.1 A busy bar holds the potential for a variety of conflict situations

Scenario 4: customer is found unconscious

You are approached by a member of the public who informs you that a man has been found unconscious in the gents' toilets. You attend the scene with another member of your security team. As your very first course of action …

Do you:

a) report the incident to the management and call for first aid to attend the scene?

b) place the man in the recovery position and leave him to sleep it off?

c) leave it in the hands of another member of staff and do nothing more?

Suggested answers

Scenario 1: refusing a customer entry

Answer C

Understand that although this is clearly the best option in this particular situation, some individuals (particularly when intoxicated) may still argue the point and even become abusive and aggressive in spite of how well-meaning you may be. The situation then has the potential to escalate into a potentially physical confrontation. For this reason, always maintain a good degree of situational awareness and control of space, and remain ever-vigilant and prepared should the situation take a turn for the worse.

Scenario 2: incident inside the venue

Answer B

Always call for assistance whenever possible. It is foolhardy to walk into any situation by yourself. Such an incident can become extremely volatile in no time. The action of separating all parties concerned and, where possible, placing them out of sight and earshot of each other is the cornerstone of de-escalation in such a situation. Here the door supervisor(s) must be sure to remain neutral and non-biased, in terms of both the argument and those involved. Just weigh up the dynamics of the situation and assess whether or not further action should be taken. As always, remain vigilant in case either party becomes physical or directs their aggression towards you or your colleague.

Scenario 3: evicting a customer

Answer A

Of course, this is the ideal. If you have a good team whose members operate well together, then this is how it can and should be done. Note, however, that you can add to this an infinite number of variables that may change the situation in some way, but you should always adhere to the basic principles of: good observation before rushing in; calling for back-up; and working as a team, with all backs observed and covered. If this approach is applied there should be minimal escalation in violence. You will also need to write up an incident report as a matter of course.

Scenario 4: customer is found unconscious

Answer A

In the event of an accident where a customer has been injured or taken ill, the venue's manager should be informed immediately. First aiders should be on hand at the scene, accompanied by two members of security and, where possible, witnesses should also be present. Depending on the seriousness and nature of the accident, an ambulance may be called. After the event, all details relating to the incident must be logged in the venue's accident book.

Even if an ambulance is not required, you should still follow the same guidelines (i.e. inform the manager, attend the scene with first aiders, in front of witnesses). From this point, advise the customer to go to hospital for a check-up and write up the accident log book. In both examples, you will not only have done the right thing, you will also have complied with procedure and covered all the angles. If a customer is taken ill and none of these measures is met and no appropriate action taken, your venue may be liable.

CHAPTER FOURTEEN

ANECDOTES

14.1 Introduction

Please note that the following accounts of incidents are included here merely as a means of giving the reader a flavour of what every door person in every city in the country has to deal with every weekend. I am sure that any door supervisor with a few years' experience under his belt could fill a manual this size with 'live situational' accounts; I'm also sure that such a manual would make very interesting reading.

I have decided to include these accounts to offer sufficient personal examples to prove that this book is based on active learning from real experience and is not a theory manual. I also want to try to give you an insight into the kind of characters you are likely to meet – and what it feels like to deal with them.

The main thing to bear in mind is that you will become effective in this precarious occupation only through your own experience. No manual can ever replace experience and even though good advice can be a very healthy supplement, the following quote says it all:

> The best preparation for an event is the event itself.
>
> *(Bruce Lee)*

14.2 The anecdotes: voices of personal experience

Rugby captain meets dry slap

Working as a doorman in various pubs and clubs I have frequently found myself in situations where I have exhausted all of my non-physical options and the only response left was a physical one. I found myself in such a situation one Friday night while working as security for a sports reunion dinner that was being held at one of the most prestigious venues in town.

At such an event you wouldn't expect any trouble, other than perhaps having to keep the odd undesirable individual from gatecrashing the party. But, as the saying goes, where there's people and huge quantities of alcohol the recipe for trouble is never that far away.

Halfway through the night I found myself facing a 17-stone under-21s rugby team captain, who had earlier been evicted via one of the fire exits to the rear of the building. By now he was drunk and full of aggressive intention. After some brief dialogue it was clear that a physical response was required, and quickly.

So I trusted my instincts and decided to pre-empt the situation: 'Look, fella, why don't you just calm down?' was the brain-engaging question that preceded an open-handed slap that his dead grandmother would have felt. The strike came from outside his peripheral vision, landing plum on the side of his face and knocking him straight to the floor instantly. He was in a semi-conscious state and took a few seconds to scramble onto all fours, and a few more to stand up. It was clear that he was in a state of shock and was no longer the combative subject I had been facing a few seconds earlier. Of course, there was every opportunity to follow up and I was prepared to do so, though in this case it wasn't necessary.

I didn't want to damage the guy, just end the threat quickly. By impacting the side of his face I simply caused him shock and pain by sending massive impact to the nerves in the facial area. I know from experience that a greater level of damage would have occurred had I struck his ear or even the side of his neck, but had the threat warranted that level of force, it would have been foolhardy to hesitate.

Of course, in the middle of any violent situation it is very hard to gauge the right amount of force required at that moment, particularly if you are in survival stress response mode, where all your decision-making abilities are severely impaired anyway, including your ability even to select a target to hit.

In such a situation you must simply hit and be prepared to continue your attack until it's over. This was one of those occasions where I felt calm enough actually to make a conscious response to the level of threat I was facing.

Awareness and an understanding of the adrenal response, along with a little experience, can help you gain control in such situations. Of course, the more severe the situation, the harder it becomes to keep hold of this elusive control, but it can be done.

LM

Attitude adjustment

I was working as a doorman at the S club in Southampton – a nice little club with an unsavoury minority. One night, within the first hour I had two violent confrontations. The first was with a bloke about 37 years old, fuelled by alcohol. A rough sort, he was posturing aggressively, spitting, and shouting insults and threats. A female door supervisor made an attempt to defuse the situation by talking him down, but this was met with an attempted assault.

At this point I intervened by shoving him back and controlling him with my fence. He moved back out of striking range and continued to posture. At this stage, another member of staff who knew this individual managed to talk him off the dancefloor area, and out into the entrance by the stairs and cloakroom.

I followed to make sure that he was leaving. Just then he started getting aggressive again and offered us both outside. It was clear that he was not going without a fight, and was too much of a threat simply to restrain, so I decided that a pre-emptive response was required.

Literally as soon as that thought had registered, the aggressor came forward with an attempted head-butt.

His forward motion was checked with a shove from my fence hand, placing him in range for a quality spike (toe-punt) kick in the groin. This lifted him off the ground and totally readjusted his attitude. From here I grabbed him and practically ran him down the stairs to the point where I had to control his descent so as not to break his neck. I got him out the door then closed it behind him, ending the situation.

About half an hour later I had to deal with another individual, about 25 years old and quite drunk. He had started an argument earlier in the evening, but had been allowed to stay after a warning. Several beers later, he started a fight with another bloke who retaliated by head-butting him, but this guy was shorter and came unstuck by cutting his own head open when his head-butt hit the taller guy in the teeth. As he staggered back, the trouble-starter went forward to attack him; as he did I spun him around into a rear choke, kicked out the back of his knee and dragged him off his feet and out of the club.

As I got him to the stairs I slammed him to the floor. At this point he was already unconscious. I calculate that he was out in about five seconds and the choke remained on for a further seven. He had turned pure white and had wet himself, so I placed him in the recovery position and he soon came round. By then the only thing that Mr 'I'll fight anyone' wanted to do was to leave as quietly as possible. I walked him out and shut the door on another confrontational situation.

LM

Finding out about yourself

On another occasion (one of many) at another club, I had the opportunity to go up against the most difficult opponent of all – myself. Two lads kicked off inside; we manhandled them out without too much of a problem, then one of them turned to me and started screaming insults. He was arm-splaying, neck pecking, showing all the signs of posturing.

I kept my fence up and attempted to calm him down, but to no avail. He continued his aggression and then moved towards me suddenly. I shoved him away telling him to 'back off' but he went for it again. As he did, my lead hand made a sudden uppercut motion under the point of his chin, snapping his head back. He dropped on the spot, falling slightly backwards into his mate who, luckily, caught his rapid descent to the pavement.

After a few seconds he came round, and said 'You're gonna be f**king sorry for that. I'm so and so's cousin, one phone call and you're f**king dead.' The family this guy was threatening me with were well-known and considered heavy artillery by some people in Southampton. The two main brothers are both ex-pro boxers, pretty good in their time. They were always in court for fighting, and considered by most to be nothing more than glorified bullies.

Now in my time working on the door I've been threatened with comebacks loads of times. I always take note of them and remain extra careful and vigilant. I was used to people dropping other people's names and reputations into the conversation, and had heard this name many times before. I've found that name-dropping is often used by those individuals who are just too insecure in their own abilities to deal with their own problems.

I went back inside and closed the door. I was positioned inside the main door so that I could let people in and out of the club. It was still quite early, with two hours to go before closing. There was a small window looking out onto the street, I could see the arsehole I had banged earlier. He was stood staring at me just the other side of the door. First, he spat blood from his split mouth at the window in an act of defiance, then he started trying to taunt me as he spoke on the phone, telling me I'd had it and that they were on their way. I met this with a completely blank expression, showing him no emotion whatsoever. This seemed to frustrate him, as he broke eye contact and moved away from the door, shouting abuse. Inside, I don't mind telling you, I felt scared – anticipation of violence is always worse than when it just kicks off and you have to act straight away. At least that way you haven't got any time to think. This guy was waiting outside for over an hour. He made a couple of calls then sat there with a smug look on his face. I was convinced that the said family were going to turn up at any minute, mob-handed.

I think the two other door staff thought so too, judging by the way they were nowhere to be seen. You need to watch out for this in such situations, especially if it's a venue that you're new to, and you don't know the door team. Good back-up is sometimes hard to find.

During the time I was stood there alone, my inner voice went to work on me: 'What are you doing here? Go home, go on, there's your car – just get in and drive off, you don't need this, you know it will get heavy when they get here.' I felt I was walking the thin line of panic, but no, I couldn't leave – I had to stay. Not because others might think less of me, but because I would think less of myself. I remembered this feeling from my school days as a bullied youngster.

This time and many times since, I have learnt that such feelings are natural, and this is how we all feel when anticipating violence (although this didn't seem to help much at the time). I had to silence the voice inside, so I countered it with thoughts of similar past experiences that I had dealt with effectively. I thought about people I knew, who had dealt with similar adversity lots of times before, those people who had inspired me to work the doors so that I would be able to deal with my own fears and personal demons.

In that moment I gained an acceptance that, whatever the outcome of this situation, I would deal with it. This is what a friend of mine by the name of Maurice Teague would call developing a 'F**k it' switch. 'Mo', as he's affectionately known, has had more experience of 'live' situations than most people could have in two lifetimes.

I knew that if these people turned up, the adrenal dump would be severe. But I would use it. I was psyched up now and mentally started to rehearse fighting at my best. I told myself I would fight for all I was worth and, win or lose, I would control my inner self, or else what had all my training been for? I made myself stay, and I beat down my negative inner opponent – who is without doubt the hardest of all to deal with. Before you can control anyone else you must first control yourself.

After what seemed like an eternity, the two lads came over to me on the door – the one I had punched apologised and offered me his hand. I took it, careful to keep my head slightly forward, in case of an attempted head-butt. He admitted that he had been bang out of order and said if the shoe had been on the other foot he would have done the same thing. A complete turnaround, it would seem. The truth is, whoever he called probably told him he deserved it and to sort out his own problems.

I shook his hand and told him I was sorry for punching him, even though I felt that he did deserve it. Then off he went with his mate. The situation itself was a minor incident, but what I went through during the waiting period in anticipation of some major violence was a true inner battle and test of character – what Geoff Thompson calls 'forge training'.

My conclusion after years of similar experiences is that fear is manageable and adrenalin can be controlled, but it will always feel the same: horrible and ugly. In the same vein it will develop your character and make you stronger in other aspects of your life. That said, although I am sick of dealing with violent and aggressive people, the majority of those who frequent the pubs and clubs we work are just fun-loving individuals out for a good time.

LM

'Easy bloody money doing the doors, mate'

A pub-cum-club called the Seven Stars in Heywood is possibly the roughest place I have even seen. One night there were three of us minding this place when these five lads came in, all strangers and all looking very rough indeed. Mind you, the dress code at the Seven Stars was easy – anything was allowed. We kept our eyes on these lads – they smelled of trouble and it was like a pressure cooker coming to life.

Finally, it kicked off: one of them punched a barmaid for serving someone else before him. We waded in, three against five, but I was lucky – I got a lovely swoop in from behind on one guy, grabbed another and dragged him into the car park. When I got back, one of the bouncers (Tony) was restraining one kid who had (it turned out later) pulled a blade, and Tony wasn't happy. When we dragged the rest out they gave us the usual 'We'll be back' Arnie-type threats.

Closing time came and, as always, I planned to take a taxi home. Tony, however, had a car in the car park and it had been trashed. As he surveyed his wrecked Cortina (which shows you it was a while ago), another car screeched into the car park from a dark corner and just ran him down. I stood there transfixed, and just managed to get one or two of the car's numbers as it sped off. The driver was the kid Tony had battered for pulling a knife.

Tony ended up in a wheelchair at 24 and now, 30-odd years later, he's still in it. He'll never walk again. Ever. Twenty quid a night we earned then, and some bastard always says when it's quiet, 'Easy bloody money doing the doors, mate.' Tell Tony that.

Dave Turton

Professionalism

Alex was a new doorman and he looked the part, but he wasn't in it for the money like some of us: he was in it for the girls. His eyes constantly roamed from girl to girl. In order to keep his mind on the job, I put him on search duty. I gave him the metal detector – a hand-held device used for detecting metal objects on a person, similar to the ones used at airports. It was a method the venue's owners preferred to the usual rubbing-down, as it was less intrusive. Alex placed himself in front of the queue. He began moving the wand down the customers' bodies, one at a time.

The flow of entry was slow. I asked 'Mof', one of the other doormen, what was causing the hold-up. Mof laughed and said, 'Alex is making everybody take off their shoes.' I went over to observe and, sure enough, every person he searched took off his or her shoes. I was beginning to think Alex had a foot fetish. People began to complain. Alex said, 'I'm just doing my job.' I observed for a minute longer, then approached him. 'Alex, why are you searching everybody's shoes?' He replied, 'Because the metal detector keeps going off when I get to their shoes.' The rest of the lads laughed when I pointed out to Alex that he had the customers standing on a metal grate.

John Skillen

Figure 14.1 All in a Friday night: Keith Harding, a door supervisor from Southampton, shows the battle scars from an incident that occurred on the door the night before we took the photos for this book

AFTERWORD

So, how can I sum up the job of door supervisor? Well, I can tell you from my own personal experience that I have found it to be one of the most character-building jobs you can have. Make no mistake, though, when you work the doors you are at times risking life and liberty, and there is no way that any two- to four-day training course will ever prepare you for that. It is my opinion that the current legislation regarding training is seriously lacking – at least in terms of the physical aspect – so learn all you can from anyone who is prepared to help you. Pay attention to everything and seek guidance from those who can help you, those who have acquired valuable experience from actually doing the job.

If all you take from this book is one thing, make it this: remember your personal safety is your priority and no amount of theory will ever give you what real experience can. Train hard in one or two physical skills that work well for you and be able to use them (assuming, of course, that we're talking about the worst-case scenario, all your non-physical options have failed and a lesser physical option just won't cut it). Learn as much as you can about your body's response to danger. Learn to expect and accept the adrenal state and make it your ally. Gain an understanding of the aggressor's body language, and the rituals of aggression and deception that he will use against you. Try to get a good team together and develop game plans for certain situations. This way you will have some idea of what you are doing under stress rather than trying to problem-solve with no direction. Last of all, and once again, remember that your safety is your priority, so stay switched on, look out for each other, don't act out of bravado or ego, and don't take any unnecessary risks.

BE AWARE

To repeat one last time what I've already said elsewhere, the tried-and-tested methods offered in this book are merely suggestions. It's important to remember that all actions carry consequences. The consequences of violence in any environment – door work included – can be tragically negative, even fatal. Heavy fines, imprisonment, serious injury and even death are all *real* possibilities. Please strive to seek non-violent solutions wherever possible – that is, after all, what real self-defence is all about.

Think smart and be confident.

Peace.

Lee Morrison, 2005

FURTHER READING

Also by Lee Morrison

Up Close, Nothing Personal. Practical Self-Protection for Door Security Staff (ISBN 1-904444-10-5). Apex Publishing, 2004, £9.99.

All of the following publications are available through Lee Morrison's website: www.urbancombatives.com.

The Bogeyman is Real. (2001) An urban combatives guide to our children's personal security. £9.99

The Combative Use of Improvised Weapons. (2004) A guide to using everyday items in drastic situations. £20.00

The Urban Combatives, Volume 1: The Game Plan. (2003) A complete manual of self-protection. £20.00

The Urban Combatives, Volume 2: Situational Combatives. (2003) A complete manual of self-protection. £20.00

The Wolverine Within. (2004) A guide to combatives for women. £20.00.

Other titles

Peter Consterdine, *Streetwise*. Protection Publications, 1996.

Edward Lewis, *Hostile Ground*. Paladin Press, 2000.

Jamie O'Keefe, *Old School – New School: A Guide to Bouncers, Security and Door Supervisors*. New Breed Publishing, 1997.

Jamie O'Keefe, *Pre–emptive Strikes for Winning Fights*. New Breed Publishing, 1998.

Peyton Quinn, *A Bouncer's Guide to Barroom Brawling*. Paladin Press, 1990.

Peyton Quinn, *Real Fighting*. Paladin Press, 1996.

Geoff Thompson, *Fear. The Friend of Exceptional People*. Summersdale Press, 2001.

Geoff Thompson, *The 3-Second Fighter*. Summersdale Press, 1997.

Geoff Thompson, *The Art of Fighting Without Fighting*. Summersdale Press, 1998.

Geoff Thompson, *The Fence, the Art of Protection*. Summersdale Press, 1998.

FURTHER TRAINING

For seminars and training please contact:

The Urban Combatives Self-Protection Association
Email: lee.morrison@getreal.co.uk
Website: www.urbancombatives.com

USEFUL ADDRESSES AND WEB LINKS

Security Industry Authority
PO Box 9
Newcastle upon Tyne NE82 6YX
Helpline: 08702 430100
Fax: 08702 430125
Website: www.the-sia.org.uk
Email: info@the-sia.org.uk

Criminal Records Bureau (CRB)
Customer Services CRB
PO Box 110
Liverpool L3 6ZZ
Information line: 0870 9090 811
Website: www.crb.gov.uk

Criminal Records Bureau (CRB) (Northern Ireland only)
Andrew Thomson T/D/Supt.
Criminal Justice Liaison & Disclosure
Criminal Justice Dept
29 Knocknagoney Road
Belfast BT4 2PR
Email: Andrew.thomson@psni.pn.police.uk

INDEX